THE
GRACE OF GOD

THE
GRACE OF GOD

By

CHARLES C. RYRIE

moody press
chicago

Paperback Edition, 1975

ISBN: 0-8024-3250-6

Printed in the United States of America

To my wife, Anne,
a gift of God's grace to me

CONTENTS

1

THE MEANING OF GRACE

I. INTRODUCTION

OH, HAD YOU BUT RECOGNIZED the grace of God in Jesus Christ our Lord."[1] The centuries that have elapsed since Augustine wrote this have in no way diminished man's need for knowing the grace of God. Christianity is distinct from all other religions because it is a message of grace. Jesus Christ is the supreme revelation of God's grace; salvation is by grace; and grace governs and empowers Christian living. Without grace Christianity is nothing.

Jesus Christ is the grace of God personified. If this be true, a number of other things are also true. First, even within the pages of the Bible the meaning of grace will vary. Since grace and truth came through Jesus Christ, the meaning of grace in the Old Testament will be different from its meaning in the New Testament. Second, we may expect the concept of grace in non-Biblical writings to be different from the Biblical concept. Third, if grace is in a Person, the doctrine of grace, though built on a word study, may extend beyond that.

These considerations pose some problems for both author and reader. If we want to understand fully what grace is, it will obviously be necessary to examine not only the Biblical material but also some non-Biblical literature. And it will be necessary not only to study the words for grace but also to survey some related ideas and doctrines. It is difficult for an author to decide how much non-Biblical material to examine and how many related ideas and doctrines to include.

Furthermore, it is not always easy to make word studies interesting to every reader. But word studies are a must if one is to have a full and correct understanding of grace. A successful meal begins with a grocery list. A proper concept is built on facts. So the facts about grace must be understood before the concept is formed; and although shopping for facts may seem to be an overlong process, let the reader be motivated and encouraged to be persistent by the thought of the delectable meal he soon will enjoy. Few doctrinal studies are so rewarding as the study of the doctrine of grace. To be able to taste, enjoy, and digest it fully is worth any effort it takes to ascertain the facts.

We will begin our study with a survey of the words for grace both in Biblical and, to a lesser extent, in non-Biblical literature. This will guide us properly in shaping our concept of grace. Next we will see the full revelation of grace in its display in the New Testament. This will lead naturally to a consideration of how grace guides the Christian's life. Right and wrong ideas concerning legalism and Christian liberty also will be discussed. Then we will want to look at some of the ideas related to salvation and the blessings salvation brings; and finally, to make our study complete, we will look at grace in the Old Testament.

The concept of grace is many-sided. This makes the word difficult to define precisely, and yet it is one of the loveliest words in our language and designates one of the most important doctrines in our theology. There is no division of doctrine that is not related in some way or another—often vitally—to the concept of grace. Inspiration, sin, salvation,

Christian living, even future things are but a few examples
of related doctrines.

Furthermore, the concept of grace is the watershed that
divides Roman Catholicism from Protestantism, Calvinism
from Arminianism, modern liberalism from conservatism.
The Roman Catholic Church holds that grace is mediated
through its priests and sacraments, while Protestantism generally does not. The Calvinist feels that he glorifies the grace
of God by emphasizing the utter helplessness of man apart
from grace, while the Arminian sees the grace of God co-
operating with man's abilities and will. Modern liberalism
gives an exaggerated place to the abilities of man to decide
his own fate and to effect his own salvation entirely apart
from God's grace, while conservatism holds that God's grace
is necessary for salvation. Man is evolving, according to liberalism, into a kind of superman who is coming to the place
where he needs no outside help, certainly not the grace of
God. However, important as the doctrine of grace is, it has
never been incorporated in any major way into the creeds of
the church, the Westminster Confession being the only exception.

As a result of the broad scope of the doctrine of grace and
its divisive effect upon the Christian Church, theologians
have tended to bend the meaning of the word *grace* to conform to the emphases of their own systems. Our English word
grace is, of course, derived from the Latin *gratia,* which is
apparently related to but not derived directly from the Greek
word for grace, *charis.* In turn, the Greek word seems to be
connected with the Semitic root *chanan,* to favor, though the
exact connection is undetermined. These facts apparently
point to some common root underlying all these words.[2] It is
noteworthy that few words are required to express grace in all
these languages. Contrast, for instance, the concept of sin,
which requires for its expression a number of different

words—sin, transgression, hypocrisy, lawlessness, deceit, and the like. The concept of grace, on the other hand, can be expressed by a few words. These few words, however, carry distinct meanings. In Hebrew there are two basic ideas, favor or good will and beauty or gracefulness. In the Greek language outside the New Testament, the principal idea is that of gracefulness or attractiveness. In the New Testament the emphasis is on the favor shown by God to man, though the ideas of attractiveness and thanks are also present. It might seem from this that it would be difficult to ascertain the exact meaning of grace in a given instance. This is not the case; for although grace bears many shades of meaning, in each specific use of the word a single idea is usually emphasized.

II. IN THE OLD TESTAMENT

The problem of the concept of grace in the Old Testament is somewhat complicated by the fact that the idea of grace as we understand it is rarely expressed. A person living today finds it difficult not to think of grace in terms of its full New Testament revelation in Christ. This he unconsciously reads back into the pages of the Old Testament. Therefore, it is necessary to make a conscious effort not to do this if one is to see the progress of the revelation of the doctrine of grace. The Old Testament does not use a single specific word to denote the concept of grace, though the several words which are used to refer to the concept are related and give background for the fuller meaning of the New Testament revelation.

A. *Chen*

The first Old Testament word to be considered is *chen* and its cognates. The verb *chanan* seems to have meant originally *to bend* or *to stoop* (I Sam. 4:19; Jer. 22:23; Lam.

4:6), and it came to include the idea of condescending favor
(Judg. 21:22). The root, which appears in proper names as
Hannah, Hanan, Hanani, Hananeel, and Hananiah, occurs
225 times in the Old Testament.

While it is true that *chen* is not an abstract concept but
an active working principle showing itself in our dealings
with others, it is equally true that this Old Testament word
for grace has little theological significance and is particularly
weak in conveying the idea of redemption. Nevertheless,
chen is used in several passages which express in a remarkable
way the redeeming favor of God toward man. After the rebellion of Israel at the giving of the law, Moses, addressing
the Lord, pressed to the fullest the favor which he had received from God as a basis for his petition for further manifestations of the divine gracious favor—*chen* (Exod. 33:13).
God did extend that favor in giving the tables of the law a
second time (Exod. 34:6-8). This was pure unmerited favor
from a superior (God) to an inferior (man).

This same divine favor is referred to by Jeremiah in a
backward look on God's deliverance of Israel from the trials
of the exodus. "Thus saith the Lord, The people which were
left of the sword found grace in the wilderness; even Israel,
when I went to cause him to rest" (Jer. 31:2).

In certain Old Testament forecasts concerning the future,
the conversion of Israel is attributed to the pouring out of
God's favor. "And I will pour upon the house of David, and
upon the inhabitants of Jerusalem, the spirit of grace and of
supplications: and they shall look upon me whom they have
pierced, and they shall mourn for him, as one mourneth for
his only son, as one that is in bitterness for his firstborn"
(Zech. 12:10). It is clear from these references that *chen*
is unexpected and undeserved, and is not secured by believing. It is the gracious condescension of a superior.[3]

The adjectival form, *gracious,* connotes the same idea of

free, undeserved favor of a superior. In twelve of the thirteen occurrences of the adjective, it is connected with mercy, often involving arresting associations. God is gracious in His consideration for the poor (Exod. 22:27). He righteously preserves the simple (Ps. 116:5), and as the compassionate Creator provides for His creatures (Ps. 111:4, 5). He is slow to anger and merciful even under provocation (Exod. 34:6; Ps. 86:15; 103:8; Joel 2:13; Jonah 4:2). In His gracious compassion He hears the entreaty of the repentant sinner and delivers (II Chron. 30:9; Joel 2:13).

Comparing *chen* with *chesed* (the other principal Old Testament word for grace), Snaith says, "It tends to carry with it, to a greater extent than does *hesed,* the idea of unmerited favor, or of supreme graciousness and condescension on the part of the giver, who is the superior. There is not the slightest obligation on the part of the superior to show this *hen.* It is all his generosity. There is no thought of any charge of harshness against him if he is not so gracious. The suppliant has not the slightest claim, nor is he in a position to do anything to enforce his claim beyond the actual petition itself."[4]

Torrance thinks this is too much of a generalization and cites instances when the Old Testament has a "tone of reprimand when favour is not showed, as to the young (Deut. 28.50), or to elders (Lam. 4:16), or to Joseph (Gen. 42:21)."[5]

However, in relation to God's showing *chen,* this thought of unmerited favor is paramount. Exodus 33:19 is particularly striking in this connection: "I . . . will be gracious to whom I will be gracious, and will shew mercy on whom I will shew mercy." Usually the favor which God bestows is in the form of redemption from enemies, evils, and sins.[6] Job recognized that even though he were righteous he would have to implore God's grace (Job 9:1 ff., especially v. 15). The psalmist prays for deliverance from the contempt of the proud (123:3), from trouble (30:10), from oppression of men (119:132-134), from desolation and affliction (9:13; 25:16), from poverty and need (86:1-3), from calamities (57:1), from devouring enemies (56:1), and from distress (4:1; 31:9).

Particularly interesting is the use of the verb in the Aaronic blessing of Israel in the name of Yahweh (Num. 6:22-26).[7] It is an immeasurable condescension that God's name should be placed on Israel in identification and blessing (Num. 6:27) and that Yahweh should make His face to shine on her (Num. 6:25).

Although *chen* has little redemptive significance, there are a few passages which connect the two ideas. "Then he is gracious unto him, and saith, Deliver him from going down to the pit: I have found a ransom" (Job 33:24). Further, the psalmist said, "Redeem me, and be merciful unto me" (Ps 26:11b). At best it can only be said that this doctrinal relationship between redemption and *chen,* grace, is but scantily revealed in the Old Testament.

B. *Chesed*

The meaning of this word is difficult to convey in English. It even defies exact description in the original, though it occurs about 250 times in the Old Testament. However, it is a word which is related to the New Testament word for grace, *charis,* even more than *chen.* "In the New Testament period *charis* would be felt to have a close relation with *chesed,* and it is evident that the associations of that word had influence in moulding the characteristic New Testament use of *charis,* which is different from any ordinary Greek use and not quite identical with the Septuagint *charis* = *chen.*"[8] Gesenius thinks the primary meaning of the root to be that of "eager and ardent desire by which anyone is led."[9] Apparently the root meaning allows for this ardent desire to manifest itself in either kindness and love or reviling and envy. In Arabic, Aramaic, and Syriac the bad meaning predominated, whereas in Hebrew the nobler idea took precedence.[10] The evil aspect of this word occurs only three times in the Old Testament (Lev. 20:17; Prov. 14:35; 25:10). Intensity of feeling is the first thing to notice about the root meaning of *chesed.*

There is a second important idea in the meaning of *chesed.* It is simply this: *chesed* involves a relationship between those involved in the act of kindness performed. This relationship is between those who are "intrinsically homogeneous" such as relatives, friends, rulers and subjects, in-laws, or hosts and guests.[11] Often such a tie was bound up in a covenant relationship, whether personal (like David and Jonathan) or corporate (like God and Israel). So important is this idea of relationship in *chesed* that it may be said that *chesed* becomes the basis on which the relationship exists and grows. In the case of Israel, who were bound to God by means of His *chesed* toward them, it meant that "the social duties and relationships of men among themselves were not regarded as merely ethical or legal, but primarily and principally religious, and in fact radically bound up with the persistent and unshakable love of God. It was this which was meant to distinguish Israel from the other nations."[12]

It becomes clear that *chesed* involved relationships between God and man in both personal and group ways and relations between fellow men. Because of this, "a *chasid* was a man who responded aright to the favor or grace of God (*chesed*)."[13]

Combining these ideas of intensity and relationship, it is plain to see that when God shows His *chesed* in a covenant relationship, His grace is firm, persistent, and steadfast. To substantiate this, Snaith has shown that out of forty-three cases when *chesed* is linked to another noun, the following is true: in twenty-three instances it is linked with fidelity, firmness, or truth; in seven with covenant; in four with righteousness; in one with prosperity; in one with stronghold; and in seven with kindness and compassion. Thus the thought of faithfulness, not the ideas of kindness and mercy, predominates in the grace relationship. "These detailed instances involve a preponderance in favor of the meaning 'firmness, steadfastness' which is often neglected. We do not desire by any means to deny the meanings 'loving-kindness, mercy' which *chesed* often has. On the contrary, our aim is to insist that these renderings are often far too weak to convey the strength, the firmness, and the persistence of God's sure love."[14]

It may help in comprehending the extensiveness of *chesed* in the Old Testament to see some of the doctrines with which it is involved.[15] This survey will demonstrate the importance of *chesed* in the warp and woof of the Old Testament. God's steadfast lovingkindness permeates the theology of the Old Testament.

Communion with God was made possible in the Old Testament by means of God's steadfast loving-kindness. For the righteous man, *chesed* was a means of entree (Ps. 5:6, 7), a precious refuge (Ps. 36:7), and the subject of contemplation in the holy place of communion (Ps 48:9).

Covenant relationships with God are regulated by *chesed*. On the divine side of the covenant the display of God's steadfast loving-kindness is guaranteed by God's faithfulness (Ps. 25:10) and righteousness (Ps. 103:17). On the human side it was expected that man would keep God's testimonies, ordinances, and commandments in a spirit of love and fear (Ps. 25:10; 103:17, 18; Deut. 7:12; Neh. 1:5). Since steadfast loving-kindness is the manifestation of covenant blessing, its withdrawal is equivalent to judgment and wrath (Jer. 16:5). God's omnipotence insures that gracious blessings shall be withheld from those who refuse to observe their covenant obligations (Ps. 62:10-12). Even though there is this human responsibility, one must not conclude that the covenants were necessarily dependent on human merit. Once God's righteous demands are met, He is free to act in grace. The enjoyment of that grace often depends on man's right relationship with God, but the exercise of that grace depends only on the steadfast loving-kindness of God.

In particular, the Davidic covenant was related to the *chesed* of God (II Sam. 7:15; I Chron. 17:13). This steadfast loving-kindness will never be removed, though David's descendants would be punished for any disobedience (Ps. 89:33, 34). Further, the *chesed* is the basis for prayer, both by the king (II Chron. 1:8; 6:14, 42; Ps. 89:49) and by the subjects on behalf of their sovereign (Ps. 61:6, 7). The ultimate fulfillment of the Davidic covenant is in the Messiah, who himself shall not be moved because of God's steadfast loving-kindness (Ps. 21:7) and whose throne for the same reason will be established forever (Isa. 16:5).

The Mosaic covenant, too, is related to the steadfast loving-kindness of God. Both the first and second giving of the tables of the law mention *chesed* (Exod. 20:6; 34:6, 7; Deut. 5:10).

Deliverance is grounded in the *chesed* of God. It forms the basis for deliverance from enemies, affliction, adversity, desert wandering, mire, deep waters, and the lowest Sheol (Ps. 6:4; 31:7, 16; 57:3; 69:13-16; 86:13; 107:8; 136:23, 24). Such deliverance is purely gracious, being available to all who seek refuge in the covenanted mercies of Yahweh through believing (Ps. 17:7; 69:13-16).

Enablement is identified with *chesed*. In Psalm 85:7 the manifestation of steadfast loving-kindness refers primarily to national revival (v. 6), though this involves conversion of heart (v. 8).

Enlightenment in the form of daily guidance in the way

(Ps. 143:8) and instruction in the divine statutes (Ps. 119:64, 124) is also provided by the steadfast loving-kindness of God.

Forgiveness was due to God's *chesed*. Under the law Moses pled for rebellious Israel about to be annihilated at Kadesh-barnea, on the basis of the greatness of God's steadfast loving-kindness (Num. 14:19). Daniel, too, made his plea on the ground of God's covenant mercies (Dan. 9:4, 13, 18). David also besought God on the basis of His *chesed* (Ps. 51:1b) after his flagrant sin.

The hope of the pious Israelite was in the Lord, with whom is steadfast loving-kindness (Ps. 130:7).

Praise is often directed to the Lord because of His *chesed*, such praise being particularly the duty of the priests (II Chron. 5:3; Ps. 13:5; 31:7; 59:16; 63:3; 86:12, 13; 89:1; 92:2; 100:5; 106:1; 107:1, 8; 115:1; 117:1, 2; 118:1-4, 9; 136:1; Ezra 3:11).

Preservation is inseparably linked with God's *chesed*. The eye of the Lord is on those who hope in His steadfast loving-kindness (Ps. 33:18), as He commands His covenant grace by day and night (Ps. 42:8). The prayer that *chesed* may preserve continually (Ps. 40:11) is not in vain. When the foot slips, *chesed* upholds (Ps. 94:18). When in a besieged city, it marvelously preserves (Ps. 31:21). In the midst of disciplinary afflictions it is a source of comfort (Ps. 119:75, 76). In the guise of storm, ice, cold or rain, it accomplishes its loving purposes (Job 37:10-13). Both Daniel, the brave, and Esther, the beautiful, were especially indebted to its influence (Dan. 1:9; Esther 2:9, 17). Indeed, all must confess that "it is of the Lord's steadfast loving-kindness that we are not consumed, because his compassions fail not" (Lam. 3:22). With God as shepherd, even the most frail of His children can exclaim: "Surely goodness and *chesed* shall follow me all the days of my life; and I will dwell in the house of the Lord forever" (Ps. 23:6).

In conclusion, we may summarize the Old Testament concept of grace as follows:

(1) There are many references to grace as the essential character of God and the imparted character of man.

(2) *Chen* is the unmerited favor of a superior to an inferior, which in the case of God as superior is expressed to man usually in temporal and occasionally in spiritual blessings and in deliverance in both physical and spiritual senses.

(3) *Chesed* is the firm loving-kindness expressed between related people and particularly in the covenants into which God entered with His people and which His *chesed* firmly guaranteed.

III. IN THE GREEK LANGUAGE

Basically the Greek word for grace, *charis*, means that which awakens pleasure or secures joy. Thus, the word can cover a wide range of meaning and is actually used in reference to bodily beauty,[16] works of art,[17] beautiful words,[18] the charm of a song,[19] the delight of the Dionysian vine,[20] the sweetness of slumber,[21] the sweetness of life,[22] the glory of victory,[23] the glory of a noble death,[24] the grace of a person,[25] and the grace that is added to virtue.[26]

To this sense of *charis* as the quality which gives pleasure is added the idea of the pleasure or joy itself, so that *charis* is sometimes synonymous with *hedone* (from which we derive the English word *hedonism*).[27] Further, there is added a psychological aspect to the Greek concept of *charis,* so that it also means the disposition or personality which is graceful, gracious, or attractive. Thus the word comes to have the meaning of graciousness, amiability, or favor.[28] Eventually, *charis* denoted a concrete act of favor or kindness which may even take the form of a gift.[29] The gratitude expressed for such a favor is also called *charis*.

While *charis* is generally used of the relations of men to

each other, it is also applied to the attitude which the gods adopt toward men. *Charis* then is sometimes used to connote divine favor toward men.[30] This favor is prayed and hoped for, and sacrifices are offered to obtain it.[31]

To summarize, *charis* had the following meanings in Greek literature:

(1) It was used objectively of that which causes a favorable regard or attractiveness; especially grace of form, gracefulness, and grace of speech, graciousness.

(2) It was used subjectively of the favorable regard felt toward a person.

(3) It was used of a definite favor.

(4) It was used of the reciprocal feeling produced by a favor granted; that is, in the sense of gratitude.

(5) It was also used adverbially in phrases like "for the sake of a thing," *charin tinos.*[32]

While *charis* has these meanings and uses in classical Greek, it should not be assumed that the concept conveyed thereby was similar to that of the New Testament. On the whole, the Greek philosophical concept of man was that he was virtuous entirely of his own merit and apart from any gift of grace. Of his own powers and will, man could aspire to virtue, and in time through practice that virtue could become a habit. There is little necessity in such a view of man for the kind of grace revealed in the New Testament.

And yet the Greek mind recognized the need for some outside help. Thus there was evident in his mythology an admission of a lack of complete sufficiency. *Charis* is used, as we have seen, of this divine favor bestowed on man and sought by man, but the gods believed in and the favors bestowed were a far cry from what is made known to the Christian through Christ.

"And so, to sum up, while on the one hand the general tendency of philosophy was to insist on the power of man to do by himself what was good and virtuous, and to attain to wisdom by the unaided powers of reason, on the other hand the popular mythology and religion in practice sought for favors and gifts from the gods, and rendered thanks to them for their largesses."[33]

IV. IN THE NEW TESTAMENT

From what has been said, it is apparent that the writers of the New Testament were heirs of a wealth of meanings for the Greek word *charis*.[34] Some of the purely Greek significations which were familiar to them do appear in their writings, but they are cast into the shadows by the blinding light of the revelation of the distinctively Christian meaning of grace. The Old Testament ideas of undeserved favor and steadfastness also appear in *charis,* but their full significance awaited the Incarnation of the Lord Jesus Christ. 'While other meanings are still current, there is a special Christian sense of the word coined under the impact of revelation to convey something quite unique."[35] "Grace and truth came by Jesus Christ" (John 1:17). Grace is the peculiar property of the Christian religion, and Christianity gave grace a meaning it never had before.

While the principal revelation of grace in our New Testament centers in the person and work of the Lord Jesus Christ, the word is used in several ways.

The classical meaning of that which affords joy, pleasure, delight, charm, or loveliness appears in at least two New Testament passages, Luke 4:22 and Ephesians 4:29.

The meaning of good will, loving-kindness, and favor is also found in several New Testament passages (Luke 1:30; 2:52; Acts 7:10, 46). Acts 7:10, where Joseph is said to have received favor in the sight of Pharaoh, is an example of the typical Old Testament concept of favor bestowed by a superior upon an inferior. In relation to God's bestowing the favor, many other New Testament passages emphasize its undeserved character (Acts 11:23; Rom. 11:6; II Cor. 4:15; 6:1; 9:14; II Thess. 1:12). On the use of *charis* in these passages, Thayer aptly comments that it refers to "the merciful kindness by which God, exerting His holy influence upon souls, turns them to Christ, keeps, strengthens, increases them in Christian faith, knowledge, affection, and kindles them to the exercise of Christian virtues."[36]

Charis is used in expressions of thanks (I Tim. 1:12; II Tim. 1:3). Notice particularly this usage in I Corinthians 10:30: "For if I by grace be a partaker, why am I evil spoken of for that for which I give thanks."[37]

Finally, *charis* is used to express certain specific benefits of grace, particularly salvation in Christ. Sometimes it covers the entire spiritual condition of the one governed by grace (Rom. 5:2; I Pet. 5:12). At other times it refers particularly to the grace of giving (I Cor. 16:3; II Cor. 8:6-7). It also includes other temporal or earthly blessings (II Cor. 9:8).

The principal benefit of *charis* is the saving grace of Christ (I Pet. 1:10, 13; II Cor. 8:9). While it is never recorded that the Lord Himself used the word *grace*, it is nevertheless perfectly clear that He was the embodiment of grace and truth (John 1:18). It was Paul who elaborated this, for it was the wonder of the grace of Christ which completely captivated that apostle. His own testimony was: ". . . last of all he was seen of me also, as of one born out of due time. For I am the least of the apostles, that am not meet to be called an apostle, because I persecuted the church of God. But by the grace of God I am what I am: and his grace which was bestowed upon me was not in vain; but I laboured more abundantly than they all: yet not I, but the grace of God which was with me" (I Cor. 15:8-10).

"God had not waited for him to win salvation. He was not left to purchase the boon of inward peace with the price of

a laborious obedience. God in His infinite grace had antic-
ipated his action. Like the father in the parable of the lost
son, He had gone to meet him while still far off. He had
plied him with love and mercy; He had offered to him the
gift of new life. He had shown Himself on the side of frail
human nature, appealing to men to enter His fellowship
through Jesus Christ."[38]

In this sense, then, grace is the favor of God in giving His
Son and the benefit to men of receiving that Son. "Grace in
the New Testament is the basic and the most characteristic
element of the Christian gospel."[39] And the one who has
believed that gospel is impelled to live a life of grace, concerned only with the doing of the will of God. This is the
true grace of God.

The New Testament also uses several words which are
closely connected with *charis*. One of these is *charitoo*, which
means *to bestow grace upon*. It occurs only in Luke 1:28 in
Gabriel's greeting to Mary as "highly favored," and in Ephesians 1:6 where every believer is said also to be highly favored
or "accepted in the beloved." The idea is that all believers
are "begraced" or overlaid with grace in Christ (following
the analogy of meanings of verbs with an -*oo* ending).[40]

A second word which is closely connected with *charis* is
charisma, a grace-gift. This word is used only by Paul in the
New Testament, with one exception (I Pet. 4:10), and it
covers the gift of salvation (Rom. 6:23), the gift of provi-
dential care (II Cor. 1:11), the gifts of marriage and conti-
nence (I Cor. 7:7), and the range of Spirit-given abilities
for service (Rom. 12; I Cor. 12; Eph. 4). These God-given
charismata are given the believer because he is an heir of
charis.

Finally, mention should be made of the relation between
mercy and grace. Mercy implies pity, whereas grace includes

the idea of favorable action toward sinners. Mercy is sometimes applied to the lower creation, but grace is used in relation to men alone (cf. Rom. 8:20-23; Job 38:41; Ps. 147:9; Jonah 4:11). " 'Mercy' is . . . but a single and subordinate aspect of *chen,* a comprehensive word, gathering up all that may be supposed to be expressed in the smile of a heavenly King looking down upon His people. This is the idea of the verb *chanan* . . . in the Aaronic benediction."[41]

Further, the opposite of mercy is misery and the opposite of grace is demerit or guilt. In planning our salvation God's mercy preceded His grace (Luke 1:78, 79; Eph. 2:4). God's love for a miserable world stems from His mercy; God's gift of His righteous Son was made necessary because of our guilt. From man's viewpoint in the outworking of his salvation, grace precedes mercy, for pardon from guilt must come before relief from misery (I Tim. 1:2; II Tim. 1:2; Tit. 1:4; II John 3). Mercy precedes in the plan; mercy follows in the provision.

To sum up: the concept of grace in the New Testament, while including all the Hebraic and classical Greek meanings, is infinitely and uniquely heightened by its association with the Saviour. The lavish gift of God in the person of His Son is the particularly New Testament meaning of grace. This is why it is quite true to say that *charis* is a word that has been raised to a higher level and filled with new meaning by our Lord Jesus Christ. His self-sacrifice is grace itself (II Cor. 8:9). This grace is absolutely free (Rom. 6:14; 5:15; Eph. 2:8), and it is that which conquers sin both in its penalty and its power (Rom. 5:12-21; 6:1-23). When that grace which was revealed in Christ is received by the believer, it then governs spiritual life by compounding favor upon favor. It equips, strengthens, and controls all phases of his life (II Cor. 8:6; Col. 4:6; II Thess. 2:16; II Tim. 2:1). Consequently, the Christian gives thanks (*charis*) to God for the riches of grace in His unspeakable gift (II Cor. 9:15). Throughout the New Testament, then, the predominant thought is the grace of God in Christ which redeems us, governs us, and gives us everlasting consolation and good hope.

2

GRACE AS SEEN IN THE
NEW TESTAMENT

GRACE IS THE PECULIAR PROPERTY of the Christian religion. Grace depends on Christianity for the realization of its full meaning and elevation to its rightful place. Grace was the focus of Christ's mission, and He himself was the embodiment of the grace of God. The development of the doctrine was largely the work of the Apostle Paul, who furnishes for us in his Epistles more material on the subject than any other New Testament writer. Altogether, then, the New Testament is the epitome of the display of the grace of God—everything prior prepares for it, and all things since are affected by it.

I. GRACE IN THE GOSPELS

The word *charis* is used in the Gospels only eleven times (Luke 1:30; 2:40, 52; 4:22; John 1:14, 16, 17; Luke 6:32, 33, 34; 17:9). In the last four references it merely means thanks. On the basis of usage we may observe several things: (1) Christ never used the word in any recorded utterance except the four instances where Luke records His using it in the ordinary sense of thanks; (2) this is not a word generally used by all the Synopticists, but only by Luke; and (3) it was recognized by the church that Christ was the full-orbed revelation of the grace of God.

In these occurrences the following meanings appear. As indicated, in Luke 6:32-34; 17:9, it simply means thanks. In Luke 1:28; 7:21, 42-43, the idea is to grant a favor, and, in these instances the favors include forgiveness, restoration of sight, and, in the case of the Virgin Mary, the privilege of bearing the Saviour. In Luke 2:40, 52, *charis* means winsomeness. However, the usage in Luke 4:22 poses a problem— "And all bare him witness and wondered at the gracious words which proceeded out of his mouth." The phrase literally reads, "words of grace," and the question is, What is the meaning of the genitive? If it is a Hebraistic genitive of quality, the phrase means "gracious words." If, however, the genitive is objective, Luke is saying that Christ spoke words about grace. This would be compatible with Lukan usage (cf. Acts 14:3; 20:32). Perhaps the form is deliberately ambiguous and we are to understand that Christ spoke gracious words about grace.

With the possible exception of Luke 4:22, the full Christian sense of grace is found in the Gospels only in John 1:14, 16-17. Here Christ is declared to be the revelation of God because He was full of grace and truth. This corresponds to Old Testament statements concerning Yahweh's character (Exod. 34:6; Ps. 25:10; 85:10; 89:14). Here, too, grace is practically made a divine attribute though its usage might be better described as the sum of those divine forces from which our salvation flows. After saving grace has come through Jesus Christ, grace is then multiplied by grace (v. 16). This is a description of the complete gratuitousness of the Christian dispensation. Under law the order was blessing for merit, but under grace it is grace instead of merit and then blessing in addition. Grace by its very nature can involve no merit.[1]

In addition to these occurrences of the words for grace, there are stories and parables in the Gospels which illustrate grace. Again, most of them occur in Luke's record. The incident of the woman in the Pharisee's house which called forth the Lord's story concerning forgiveness of sinners (Luke 7:36-50) ; the parable of the great supper (Luke 14:16-24) ; the parables of the lost sheep, lost coin, and lost son (Luke 15) ; the parable of the Pharisee and the publican (Luke 18:9-14) ; and the detailed account of the repentant thief on the cross (Luke 23:39-45) all give evidence of the fact that the grace of Christ toward sinners had evidently made a deep impression on Luke. Other incidents recorded by Gospel writers which tell of the grace of Christ are: the parable of the laborers in the vineyard (Matt. 20:1-16), the parable of the marriage feast (Matt 22:1-14), and the conversation with the Samaritan woman (John 4:6-26).

Although the Gospels reveal the One who Himself was the revelation of God's grace, there is in them no theological development of the doctrine. Even John, in the first chapter of his account, only approaches such a development. For the most part the word *grace* is used in relatively nontechnical and ordinary Hebraic ways. It remained for Paul to systematize the doctrine and associate the word with all that God has done for man in Christ. The Gospels reveal the Lord of grace and everywhere indicate that the saving initiative is with God, but Paul is the principal divine agent for interpreting the full meaning of the life and death of Christ in terms of God's grace.

II. GRACE IN THE ACTS

As in the case of other doctrines, the book of Acts furnishes a bridge for the doctrine of grace from the general and casual use in the Gospels to the technical and fully developed use in the Epistles. The Hebraistic sense of favor continues to be found in the book (2:47). In two instances it is in reference to Old Testament events (7:10, 46) ; and in two others it is used in connection with a nonreligious favor (24:27; 25:3).

Early in the ministry of Paul we find *charis* being used as a synonym for the gospel and its results (13:43). It is used specifically of the new message in other places too (14:3; 20:24, 32). These references show that the early church realized that the distinguishing feature of the gospel was grace and that it was centered in Jesus the Messiah.

But the grace of God was not only considered the content of the gospel; it was also viewed as the means of bringing it to men (15:11; 18:27). These two references relate the grace of God to the inclusion of Gentiles in God's plan of salvation. It is by the grace of the Lord Jesus and not by the law, the Jerusalem council decided, that Jews are saved in the same way as non-Jews are.

Certain gifts are also attributed to grace in the book of Acts. These are not gifts unto salvation but gifts that come after salvation. Believers' lives exhibited the grace of God in visible ways. All believers in Jerusalem in the very early days felt the grace of God upon them (4:33). Changed lives were evidently the clear manifestation of the grace of God at work in Antioch, for when Barnabas came from Jerusalem to examine the work, he saw the grace of God (11:23). Again, the use of the word here involves Gentiles' being admitted to the divine blessings. Nor was there mention of miraculous signs in Antioch, as at Jerusalem; rather, the grace of God was evident in the changed lives of believers. Grace also accounted for the change in the life of Stephen (6:8 A.S.V.), who was given power to perform miracles as the apostles did. Furthermore, grace was regarded as necessary equipment for missionary work, particularly the work of keeping God's emissaries safe (14:26; 15:40). Thus, grace's gifts are changed lives, the performance of miracles, safekeeping; and they are given to both Jewish and Gentile believers.

To summarize: in the book of Acts *charis* continues to be used in the general Old Testament sense of boon or favor, but it also comes into its own specific Christian use. It became equivalent to the message, it was regarded as the means of bringing that message to human hearts. It included Gentiles, and it resulted in bounteous gifts from God.

III. GRACE IN THE PAULINE EPISTLES

The most important stage in the development of the New Testament doctrine of grace is the writing of the Pauline Epistles. For Paul, grace was fundamental to all his thinking. Paul was not interested in the ideas involved in grace "as subjects of detached speculation, even when he discusses them in language which sounds abstract. They are for him vital realities of the Christian faith, in the light of the resurrection of the Lord. What the Lord had done and what the Lord demanded was summed up in 'grace.' It was because he had verified this in his own experience and because he found himself obliged at various points to explain and apply it during the course of his mission, that he wrote as he did upon the subject, always with a more or less practical and direct aim, yet also from a central conviction."[2] On the Damascus Road there burst on the mind of Paul two great facts: all is of grace, and grace is for all. These great truths he propagated with unflagging zeal in life and ministry.

All of the Pauline Epistles open and close with a mention of grace. Such a salutation at the beginning was a customary practice, but Paul's use of it was not ordinary. The conventional Greek letter opened with *chairein,* which included both the ideas of cheerfulness and thankfulness. In a certain sense, however, Paul created a new form of greeting when he used the noun *charis* instead of the verb, and in combination with "peace." The greeting became a prayer and the order of the words indicated that God's favor in grace was the basis for the enjoyment of peace by the believer. The conventional closing of a Greek letter was "farewell," *errosthai* (cf. Acts 15:29; 23:30). The use of *charis* in this way was an innovation. "That Paul struck out a fresh conclusion to the Christian letter was more than a stylistic idiosyncrasy; it indicates the dominant place of 'grace' in his religious vocabulary, and also the fact that this was recognized by his churches as characteristic of his own message."[3]

A. First and Second Thessalonians

In the correspondence with the Thessalonian church, which by many is still considered the earliest of Paul's letters, grace is mentioned specifically only twice in the second letter, except for the customary opening and closing greetings. However, the idea is very strong in the first letter. Election, which elsewhere is so definitely related to the gracious action of God, is the theme of the opening chapter (1:4). In the second letter Paul attributes to grace all the evidences of their faith and love, especially in suffering (1:12). The desired end of grace is the glory of God. In the meantime, in the trials of life the Lord gives encouragement, hope, and stability through grace (2:16-17). Grace would keep the believers from wavering in the midst of persecution by directing their attention to the hope of the future.

B. First Corinthians

In I Corinthians the uses of *charis* fall into four categories. First of all, Paul uses it of that which God did when He apprehended him on the Damascus Road. "But by the grace of God I am what I am: and his grace which was bestowed upon me was not in vain; but I laboured more abundantly than they all: yet not I, but the grace of God which was with me" (I Cor. 15:10). It was grace which changed the course of his life and which motivated him to more abundant service. Second, Paul uses *charis* of enablement for acceptable Christian service. The verse just cited also includes this idea. Further, Paul attributed to grace his wisdom as a masterbuilder (3:10). Third, Paul uses the word in the ordinary sense of thanks (10:30). Finally, grace is used to encompass the whole range of spiritual gifts present in the Corinthian assemblies (1:4). What these were is delineated in the twelfth chapter under the related word *charisma*, grace-gift (12:4, 9, 28, 30, 31). This is a word used only by Paul in the New Testament with the exception of I Peter 4:10, and it is used to describe God-given abilities for service. In addition to these specific instances, Paul writes in the opening chapters of this Epistle of the elective purposes of God as evidences of His grace. These are revealed through the foolishness of the thing preached and the calling out of the weak, despised, and foolish things of this world (1:18-29). Again, as in II Thessalonians 1:12, this action of God's grace is for the purpose of glorifying Himself.

C. Second Corinthians

In II Corinthians grace is related to five categories. First, saving grace is spoken of (6:1), and, as in I Corinthians 15:10, it is seen as issuing in service. Second, Paul speaks of enabling grace. In 4:15 he relates it to the glory of God through standing fast in persecution. If this Epistle was written after the uproar at Ephesus and hounding by the Jews in Macedonia (Acts 19:23—20:3), it particularly emphasizes the power of enabling grace. The other instance of this use also relates to difficulty (12:9). Paul's thorn in the flesh, whatever it was,[4] enabled him to verify, as he could not otherwise have done, the grace of God. The word translated "sufficient" stands in the emphatic position in the sentence, which literally reads, "It is enough to you to have my grace."

Third, grace (*charisma*) is considered as a boon (1:11). Apparently Paul is here speaking of some temporal deliverance from difficulty, and he calls this a gift of grace. Fourth,

Paul speaks of *charis* as the sphere of his life (1:12). It is set in contrast to worldly cunning and is declared to be the rule of his conduct both in the outside world and among the Corinthians. Grace in this instance is the ruling and controlling principle by which the apostle's ministry and life were guided. "Grace is the foil to astuteness or calculation; primarily it is opposed to any consideration of self in his ministry."[5]

The fifth and most distinguishing use of grace in this Epistle (and one of the most distinctive in the entire New Testament) is its use in connection with the giving of money (8—9). This is not illogical, for if grace in the New Testament is particularly displayed in the gift of God's Son, the word can well be used to express the unselfish action involved in the gifts of men. God's own gift should inspire and be the ethical motivation for the gifts of men. Grace means giving for men as well as for God.

A number of facets of the relationship between grace and giving are seen in this central New Testament passage on the subject. First of all, the source of giving is grace bestowed (8:1). Giving is due to grace. Men by nature want to receive; Christian men by new nature want to give. Second, the particular act of giving is called grace (8:4, 6, 7, 19). The actual collection for the starving believers in Judea was designated a grace. Third, the great example for giving is the grace manifested in the gift of Christ (8:9). The grace of Christ involved the self-renunciation of His heavenly privileges in order to carry out God's saving purpose toward man. The riches which His poverty brought to man include reconciliation, gifts of the Spirit, hope for the future, and all the blessings of the Christian life. You know, Paul says, that this is all due to the grace of Christ. Now, because you know, follow His example and be generous toward other Christians.

Finally, the reward of giving is added grace (9:8). Gen-

erosity will be rewarded by additional grace. This undoubtedly includes sufficient material provision for the giver as well
as the development of his character. In other words, God
gives or "begraces" the giving Christian with sufficient money
and character in order that he may continue to want to and
be able to give. Paul concludes this section, however, by re-
minding his readers again that this grace of giving is entirely
due to the work of the grace of God in them (9:14).

D. *Galatians*

As one would expect from the historical setting of the book,
grace in Galatians is primarily related to the message of the
gospel. The Judaisers had perverted the gospel by adding
circumcision as a requirement for salvation and fleshly works
as a necessity for sanctification. To support themselves in
their position they appealed to the historic faith of the Old
Testament, to their prestige as coming from headquarters in
Jerusalem, and to the natural inclinations of everybody's
flesh to want to earn a reward. In answer to these arguments,
Paul pointed out that the Old Testament promise of an inheritance to Abraham (an indisputable test case for any Jew)
was given by grace (cf. 3:18, where the verb is used—"God
gave it by grace to Abraham by promise"). Whatever the law
required by way of circumcision could not annul the promise,
which was given by grace and conditioned only on faith.
Furthermore, Paul sets in sharp contrast any righteousness
which might have come by the law with the righteousness
which comes by grace through faith (2:21). To preach righteousness on any other basis than grace is to frustrate the grace
of God, for it negates the value of the death of Christ. This is
a strong statement, but it clearly reveals the sharp antithesis
in the apostle's mind between God's free grace in Christ and
the meritorious works of any system, particularly the Mosaic
law.

Over against the assumed prestige which the Judaisers claimed because they came from Jerusalem, Paul places his own apostolic calling. This calling, he declares, was not dependent on the other apostles, but was the direct action of the risen Christ. Furthermore, his calling was "through his grace" (1:15) and for the purpose of revealing Christ in Paul and preaching Him among the Gentiles. This grace calling unto apostleship was effected on the Damascus Road, and Paul makes much of the fact that, after that experience, he did not confer with the other apostles. Therefore, his apostleship was the direct result of grace. This work of God in Paul's life was affirmed by the Jerusalem leaders many years later (perhaps Galatians 2 is to be related to the Jerusalem council of Acts 15). James, Peter, and John recognized the grace of apostleship which was given Paul and showed their recognition by giving him the right hand of fellowship (2.9). Here again grace is used as a synonym for apostleship, and in the heat of the Galatian controversy it was a very significant synonym.

Finally, the Judaisers appealed to the natural inclinations of human flesh to want to merit acceptance before God. This works principle of justification is denounced in no uncertain terms and set in direct opposition to the grace of God. "I marvel," the apostle says, "that ye are so soon removed from him that called you into the grace of Christ unto another gospel: which is not another; but there be some that trouble you, and would pervert the gospel of Christ" (Gal. 1:6-7). To accept this perversion, which is later defined as seeking to be justified by the Mosaic law, is to fall from grace (5:4). Since grace is God's way of justification, to seek any other way is to fall from the right way. The grace way does not need supplementation by the law and particularly by circumcision. Furthermore, the grace way produces proper ethical conduct because it originated in the unselfish, loving gift of Christ. Grace, the work of Christ, and the gospel are completely interchangeable terms in the argument of chapter five.

Thus in the Galatian Epistle, we find that grace is the answer to all the arguments of the Judaisers, because, as Paul says elsewhere, "Christ is the end of the law for righteousness to everyone that believeth" (Rom. 10:4). Perhaps in no other Epistle is the particular display of grace in the work of Christ so clearly revealed as in Galatians. All of grace (not by law) and grace for all (even uncircumcised Gentiles).

E. *Romans*

In Romans, the most theological of Paul's Epistles, we find the most systematic development of the doctrine of grace. This is to be expected, since the heart of Paul's message was the gospel, the power of God unto salvation, and since grace is used as a synonym for gospel and salvation. In the introduction to the book Paul speaks of the grace of salvation and calling of apostleship which he himself had received for the purpose of bringing others to the place of obedience to the faith (1:5). After a rather lengthy introduction (since the apostle was unknown personally to his readers), he launches into the development of the theme. Salvation is first painted against the backdrop of sin, for in seeing what sin has done, we can more greatly appreciate what grace has done. The thought of righteousness in 1:17 immediately suggests the somber effects of sin. The result is the lengthy survey in this first section (1:16–3:20) of the moral character of mankind, in which Paul shows that all men, Jews and non-Jews alike, have come short of God's standard.

When Paul turns from the negative to the positive (3:21–5:21), there is an immediate mention of grace (3:24). In the space of a few short verses most of the key words of the

Christian faith are mentioned—righteousness, faith, justification, grace, redemption, propitiation, and remission. What is the relation of grace to these concepts? "Being justified freely by his grace through the redemption that is in Christ Jesus" (Rom 3:24). Justification is the act of declaring a person righteous. This is the ultimate goal of God's work in salvation—that He may declare before all the universe a sinner to be righteous. The mode by which this is accomplished is "freely," or without any cause in us that could demand or require or merit it (cf. John 15:25). "By his grace" indicates the origin or impetus for this action which leads to justification, and that action is the redemptive work of Christ. Though unmerited by us, God exercised His grace toward us by taking the initiative in giving His Son to die that men through faith might be justified. All this is due to grace.

Paul then proceeds to enforce his argument by an incontrovertible illustration, the faith of Abraham (4:1-25). Twice in the chapter he emphatically states that righteousness came to Abraham *kata charin,* according to the standard of grace (vv. 4, 16). Abraham was not a workman who gained righteousness as one might receive wages for work done, but he was a suppliant who received by grace what he did not deserve. In this way his faith was imputed for righteousness, and in the same way God is the justifier of him who believes in Jesus.

It is clear, then, that grace as used by the apostle is not limited to the gift of Christ, but it also includes and stands for the whole new relationship into which the believer is brought. Indeed, this is the meaning of the next use of *charis* in the Epistle (5:2). The believer is said to "stand in grace," a phrase which comprehends in the broadest sense the resultant position which grace provided. " 'Justification' is not permission to wait in an antechamber, it is admission to the inner presence of God."[6] Grace not only introduces us to the presence of God, but it also causes us to rejoice in the hope of the future consummation of our redemption, to be patient in present tribulations, and to experience the love of God shed abroad in our hearts. Grace has constituted the believer in a state of grace.

The section closes with the statement of contrasts between Adam and Christ, offense and gift, death and life, transgression and obedience, condemnation and justification, and sin and grace all set in sharp contrast. The state into which grace brings us is a gift (v. 15), it is given in abundance (v. 17), and it reigns unto eternal life by Jesus Christ our Lord (v. 21).

That perfect righteousness which is imputed to us by grace is imparted to and appropriately by us so that it becomes our own. This sanctified living is the subject of the third major section of the Epistle (6:1—8:39). Actually, except for the discussion concerning Israel in chapters nine through eleven, it is the subject of the remainder of the letter.

Sanctification too is related to grace (6:1, 14-15), for being under grace is the basis for holy living. The law brings the knowledge of sin (7:7), but grace brings freedom from sin and victorious living. This aspect of Christian living under grace will be discussed in detail in chapter five.

In the so-called parenthetical section concerning Israel (9-11) Paul uses grace two times and in connection with the salvation of the remnant of Jewish people (11:5-6). That Jews were saved then was because of grace, and Paul himself was one of those who had experienced it. Again, as in the test case of Abraham in chapter four, works and grace are set in antithesis to each other (v. 6).

In the final section of the Epistle, Paul attributes the giving of spiritual gifts to grace. This he considered true in his own case (12:3) and in the case of other believers (12:6).

Grace means for the Christian a certain combination of spiritual gifts which are to be exercised in a particular ministry toward others.

In summary, grace in Romans includes the grace of apostleship (or service), grace unto justification, grace as the sphere of sanctification, electing grace as seen in the Jewish remnant, and the grace which effects the bestowal of spiritual gifts. It is plain to see that every area of the Christian life is built upon the unmerited favor of God as set free in the gift of His Son.

F. *The Prison Epistles*

The uses of the word *charis* in Ephesians may be classified under grace for salvation, grace for service, and grace for speech. Saving grace is a reciprocal arrangement. God in the giving of His Son offers redemption and remission of sins according to the riches of His grace (1:7), and this salvation is emphatically declared to be apart from works (2:5, 8). In turn, the man who has been the recipient of this unmerited favor is expected to glorify the grace of God (1:6; 2:7). But this magnifying of the grace of God on the part of the believer is something for which man can claim no credit, for the only reason he can show off the grace of God now or in eternity is simply because he received it. God bestowed it on him as an act of grace for which he can claim no credit. It is all of grace.

Grace for service is illustrated by the calling of Paul (3:2, 7-8). In his case the service which God called him to do was to make known the dispensation of the grace of God. This mystery, a thing not revealed in the Old Testament but revealed in the New, was simply that "Gentiles should be fellow-heirs, and of the same body, and partakers of his promise in Christ by the gospel" (3:6). His apostleship concerned especially the fact that grace was for *all*.

But all Christians too are called to serve, and the provision that makes their service possible is due to grace. The discussion concerning gifts is prefaced by the statement that "unto every one of us is given grace according to the measure of the gift of Christ" (4:7). The purpose of this varied distribution of grace-gifts is the perfecting of the saints by their growth into the knowledge of the truth (vv. 12-13). Since true Christian service can only be carried out through the proper exercise of spiritual gifts, and since spiritual gifts are grace-gifts, all Christian service is the result of the grace given "according to the measure of the gift of Christ" (4:7).

In particular Paul deals in Ephesians with the grace necessary to please God in our speech (4:29). Worthless speech should be replaced by speech that will minister grace to those who hear. Whatever we say should be as a favor or boon to the one who hears. The point here is simply that our speech should benefit the hearers. As explained by the context of this verse, this means that speech which ministers grace will be useful (in contrast to "corrupt" or useless communication), pleasing to the Holy Spirit, and devoid of any of the characteristics listed in verse 31. Speech which ministers grace has to be spoken with grace, for there is no other way to control the tongue (cf. Col. 4:6).

As would be expected because of their being written so closely together, the references to grace in Colossians are similar to those in Ephesians. Grace is a synonym for "the word of the truth of the gospel" (1:5-6). As is Paul's emphasis everywhere, so here saving grace will exhibit itself in a fruitful life. Grace in connection with speech is also mentioned in the Epistle (4:6). Here, however, the emphasis is more on the content of the speech than on the effect of it on the hearers, as in Ephesians. Our speech is to be with grace. This probably is to be understood in two ways. We should speak realizing that we merit no favor in God's sight and that all we are or hope to be is because of His grace.

Further, *charis* in this verse may have an overtone of the simple meaning of thanks. Therefore, combining these two ideas, our speech should always show consciousness of the unmerited favor bestowed on us and every word should exude our thankfulness for that grace.

The new relationship of grace mentioned in Colossians is grace in connection with singing and praise (3:16). The singing (as at the love-feasts) of psalms (accompanied music), hymns (song of praise), and spiritual songs (songs inspired by the Holy Spirit) is to be from hearts filled with grace. As with gracious speech, gracious singing means singing in the realization that all that we have or are or hope to be is due to the unmerited favor of God, and singing with thankfulness for that position in grace which grace has provided.

The short letter to Philemon contains no uses of *charis* except the customary greeting and benediction, as previously indicated (vv. 3, 25).

The only occurrence of the word (outside of the customary opening and closing) in Philippians is in 1:7: "Even as it is meet for me to think this of you all, because I have you in my heart; inasmuch as both in my bonds, and in the defence and confirmation of the gospel, ye all are partakers of my grace." The Philippian church had been companions in Paul's grace not only because they shared the same salvation but also because they shared their money and partook of sufferings together. With this church Paul had a strong bond—a bond which was woven of common salvation, common sustenance, and common suffering.

G. *The Pastoral Epistles*

The prominence given to grace in the Pastoral Epistles is much less than in the other Pauline writings.[7] With one exception all the references (except the usual opening and closing ones) are to saving grace. The exception is II Timothy

2:1, where the power of the position into which the believer has been brought by grace is made the basic of the exhortation. The other references refer to some aspect of salvation. In thinking of his life in Judaism in contrast to his present position in Christ, Paul's own testimony was, "The grace of our Lord was exceeding abundant with faith and love which is in Christ Jesus" (I Tim. 1:14). Two other references relate grace to the appearing of Christ (II Tim. 1:9; Titus 2:11), the distinguishing feature of grace in its New Testament display, and the final reference connects justification and grace (Titus 3:7). In the Titus 2:11 context there is that oft-repeated emphasis on the manifestation of the effects of the appearing of Christ in the believer's fruitful and self-denying life.

In summarizing this survey of Paul's use of *charis*, certain observations may be made. First, the origin of his concept may be traced to the Damascus Road experience. As a Pharisee Paul was schooled in the idea that everything was earned. When the risen Christ appeared to him, He showed the Pharisee that what he had been seeking by works was a gift of grace. Justification, which the law of Moses could not provide, was now given him through the grace of Christ (cf. Acts 13:39). Paul was also keenly aware throughout his entire life and ministry that his calling to apostleship and his strength for discharging it were due to grace (I Cor. 15:10; Gal. 1:15; I Cor. 3:10).

Second, whenever Paul writes of grace he invariably writes of the grace of God. In the Pauline Epistles we do not find reference to the favor of men toward men but only of God toward men. He recognized that God was the fountainhead of all grace. Furthermore, Paul invariably links the manifestations of the grace of God with the appearing of Jesus Christ. This is the distinguishing feature of the New Testament display of grace, and with His appearing and because of His work, that which the law could not provide, justification, is freely bestowed upon all who believe. All of grace and grace for all.

Third, Paul's conception of grace was a multifarious one. The grace of God was for Paul the grace of his Lord Jesus Christ. Grace was for him centered in the self-sacrifice of Christ (II Cor. 8:9; Gal. 2:20). Furthermore, grace was conceived of as absolutely free (Rom. 3:24; 5:15; 6:14; Eph. 2:8). Also it is a sin-conquering power both in the realm of salvation and in the realm of sanctification (Rom. 5:12-21; 6:1-23). Grace is offered to all men (both Jew and Gentile), though no gift is really given until it is received and only those who believe receive the grace of Christ. Finally, grace in Paul's thought represents the sum-total of all the believer's blessings (Eph. 1:7; cf. 3:8). Grace saves, justifies, calls, sanctifies, equips for service, strengthens, promotes liberality, gives good hope, and controls singing and speaking. Certainly the church owes to the Apostle Paul the preeminence given in the New Testament to the concept of grace.

IV. GRACE IN HEBREWS

Variety and uniqueness of usage are the chief characteristics of the use of *charis* in the book of Hebrews. The word appears only seven times, but these occurrences show a range of depth and comprehension on the part of the author. The Epistle was written as a warning to backsliders in the faith and compromisers with Judaism. *Charis* touches the heart of this matter.

In asserting the superiority of Christ, the author compares Him with Old Testament prophets, angels, Moses, and Joshua. In climaxing the comparison with angels, he declares that Christ was crowned with glory and honor because of having suffered on the cross, in order by God's grace to taste death for every man (2:9). In other words, the grace of God provided that redemption which the law could not provide, and in so doing it became the route to the crowning of Christ. The phrase "by the grace of God" "covers the divine motive, the mission of the Son, the very methods of suffering, and the wide object in mind."[8]

At the conclusion of the first section of the book, which contains these comparisons, the writer serves warning on his readers that they must not fail to enter into the rest which God has provided. The experience of the Israelites in the wilderness is intended to be a strong reminder of the need of accepting the promises of God. Set against this background, the contrasts and expressions of the final verse are interesting: "Let us therefore come boldly unto the throne of grace, that we may obtain mercy, and find grace to help in time of need" (4:16). Grace is set in the position of the regal splendor of sovereign power. Grace enthroned makes the throne of God a throne of grace, and because it is such the believer may expect to find grace to help in time of need. While the broader context concerns the dealings of God with Israel, the immediate context encourages the Christian by assuring him that he has in Christ a sympathetic high priest. Therefore, whatever may be the difficulties he is called on to bear, the Christian can be assured that they originate from a throne of grace and that while in them he can be sustained by grace from that throne.

In another warning in the book the writer employs the unique phrase *the Spirit of grace*. This is the only undisputed example in the New Testament which links the Holy Spirit and grace (there is a question as to whether Romans 1:4 refers to the Holy Spirit or to Christ's natural spirit). But here clearly the Spirit is declared to be the one who applies grace to the believing heart in the work of regeneration. Thus, to reject the gift of the Son of God is to do despite to the Spirit of grace.

The remaining instances of grace in the book all relate in one way or another to the Christian life. The entire progressive nature of the Christian life is called grace in 12:15, and the readers are warned not to lag behind what God wants to do for them by way of growth and progress. Furthermore, in order to be able to grow and thus to serve God acceptably, it is necessary to have the help of grace (12:28; 13:9). The latter reference may indicate that some of the readers were trying to make the matter of eating or non-eating of meats a means of grace. The heart must be established with the sense of God's goodness, not with external things. The sacrifice of the Lord, not the ritual meal, is what confirms the heart.

The book also contains one outstanding passage in which, although the word *grace* does not appear, law and grace are sharply contrasted (12:18-24). It is an elaboration of John's declaration that "the law was given by Moses, but grace and truth came by Jesus Christ" (John 1:17). In this paragraph the writer to the Hebrews incorporates several distinct contrasts—Moses and Christ, Mount Sinai and Mount Zion, death and life. The old dispensation is illustrated with the frightening sight of the giving of the law on Mount Sinai. Even Moses reacted with fear and trembling, for the law of itself could give no assurance of life. The Christian, by contrast, has been given a place in the heavenly city, and the grace of God set free through the death of Jesus, the Mediator of the New Covenant, has accomplished it all.

V. GRACE IN THE GENERAL EPISTLES

Except for I Peter, an epistle of grace, the uses of the word are scarce in the General Epistles.

James uses the word only twice (4:6). This is the climax to an exhortation concerning serving two masters. There was evidently much bickering in the assemblies due to divided allegiance. This also resulted in unanswered prayer for the believers, and it was grievous to God, who desires to possess all of us. To the one who gives undivided allegiance to the Lord, the Lord gives more grace. This undoubtedly includes, in this instance, more answers to prayer, as well as continuous supply of material needs. The quotation from Proverbs 3:34 in the latter part of the verse and in I Peter 5:5 are the only quotations from the Septuagint in the New Testament which include "grace." Although 4:6 contains the only uses of *charis,* James certainly expresses the Old Testament idea of favor or boon in 1:17.

In the second letter of Peter the word occurs only at the beginning (1:2) and end (3:18). The latter reference is not like the usual benediction. "Grow in grace" is a very expansive use of the word. It means that everything in the life of the Christian from start to finish is the gracious, unmerited gift of God, and that a full understanding of grace requires growth in it. The close association of growth in grace with knowledge of Jesus Christ shows again that the New Testament uniformly connects grace with Christ.

In II John the only occurrence is in the greeting.

In the Epistle of Jude "grace" is used again for the entire message of Christianity, with special emphasis on its moral implications. Some had come into the church with antinomian doctrines. This Jude describes as "turning the grace of God into lasciviousness" (v. 4). Jude considered these false teachers to be unredeemed people (v. 19), for the message of grace when received results in a holy life.

First Peter is in a very real sense an Epistle of grace. Indeed, this is by the writer's own statement the theme of the letter (5:12). Some of Peter's uses of grace are quite normal. Grace is mentioned in relation to grace-gifts (4:10), the only non-Pauline reference to *charismata.* The connection is simply this: the proper exercise of gifts will exhibit the grace of God both in the fact that ministry is given to men and in the con-

tent of that ministry—revealing Jesus Christ. Grace is also
used in reference to Christian living (5:5, 10). It is given to
the humble and it is linked with suffering. In 3:7 Peter uses
charis with an unclear meaning. "Heirs together of the grace
of life" may have physical or spiritual connotations. It might
mean that to husband and wife has been given the grace,
favor, of being able to bring into being a new physical life.
Or the reference may be to the grace of spiritual salvation of
which the Christian couple are heirs.

The other two instances of grace in I Peter are rather un-
usual (as is 3:7 if understood in the physical sense). The
first is the use of *charis* as the content of Old Testament
prophecy (1:11). However, the reference only reflects the
fact that the prophets understood that God would act in
grace in a coming day. That this grace was to be revealed
in Jesus Christ they did not clearly see, nor does Peter say
that they did. Generally speaking, Old Testament prophets
saw little more than that Gentiles would be included in God's
gracious dealings with mankind.

The other unique use of "grace" is eschatological (1:13).
Here grace is viewed as a blessing to be received at the
second coming of Christ. In the other New Testament books
grace is not made the object of hope as it is here, and particularly in Paul's Epistles it is wrapped up with the work
of Christ and the present life of the Christian. But that grace
is an eschatological blessing is no surprise, for grace is salvation and salvation is not fully culminated until the second
coming of Christ. But this emphasis is distinctively Petrine.

VI. SUMMARY

From this survey of the display of grace in the New Testa-
ment, certain conclusions may be drawn by way of summary.
First, *charis* was specified and transfigured by the coming of
Christ. He is revelation of the grace of God in a way never

experienced formerly. This is the outstanding feature of the New Testament display of grace. Second, though the character of grace was changed immediately by the coming of Christ, the use of the word *grace* changed more gradually. In the Synoptic Gospels and in the Acts it was still used with Old Testament meanings. Third, the Apostle Paul was the chief human instrument which effected this change. Since it is neither the first nor last of his Epistles—but rather in the middle group—in which the word is used most often, we might further conclude that the Galatian controversy was an important experiential factor in the forging of the expression of his doctrine of grace. However, the truth was previously revealed to him on the Damascus Road (Eph. 3:3; Gal. 1:15). He did not evolve it because of the Galatian trouble; he merely used and systematically expressed what God had already revealed to him through Jesus Christ. Fourth, the New Testament offers grace to all, though it recognizes an election according to grace. This is in contrast to the Old Testament doctrine which usually restricts even the offer of grace to God's elect people Israel.

The grace of God in the New Testament is His unmerited favor in the gift of His Son, who offers salvation to all and who gives to those who receive Him as their personal Saviour added grace for this life and hope for the future. Every facet of this broad conception of grace is rooted in the fact "that in the New Testament the 'grace of God' is 'the grace of the Lord Jesus Christ.' "[9]

3

LIVING UNDER GRACE

GRACE IS AN INSEPARABLE PART of Christian living. Not only
has the grace of God been gloriously manifested in the gift
of Christ, but grace vitally affects the life of the believer in
Christ. To discover the detail and extent of this effect is the
purpose of this chapter.

In many places the New Testament writers emphasize the
ramifications of grace in respect to Christian living. This is
perhaps most forcibly done in Titus 2:11-14. Here the
writer's emphasis, though not unrelated to the Incarnation,
is on the disciplinary ministry of grace. The grace of God
hath appeared—the verb is aorist and refers to the specific
act of the Incarnation. God's grace was so definitely manifested in the gift of Christ that, relatively speaking, there had
been no previous and there will be no subsequent displays of
His grace, since that one completely outshines all other displays of God's favor. However, basic as the Incarnation is
(and without it there would be no grace for Christian living),
Paul's point here is that grace teaches the believer how to live.
The verb *teaching* encompasses the whole concept of growth—
discipline, maturing, obedience, progress, and the like. This
involves denial of improper things and direction into proper
channels. These five terms—ungodliness, worldly lusts, so-

berly, righteously, godly—do not describe the content of grace
teaching so much as they indicate the object and purposeful
goal of that teaching. And this intent is, according to this
passage, the ultimate purpose of the Incarnation of Christ.
He came to display the grace of God in the changed lives of
His people. The final cause of the revelation of the grace of
God in Christ is not creed but character.

What is the Christian character which is the goal of grace
teaching? Although it involves many details, ultimately it is
the character of Christ. This is implied even in this passage.
All good teachers reproduce themselves in their pupils. Grace
is our teacher, but New Testament grace is essentially Christ.
Therefore, to say that grace teaches with the intent of repro-
ducing in believers that same grace is to say that Christ teaches
in order to reproduce Himself in the life of the Christian.
Living soberly, righteously, and godly is the imitation of
Christ.

How does grace reproduce grace? Again Paul gives us the
answer—by placing the Christian under grace (Rom. 6:14).
In this passage, which deals with the Christian's sanctification, being "under grace" is set in sharp contrast to being
"under law." It is perfectly evident that "under law" and
"under grace" are complete opposites, and it is equally clear
that the only way for a Christian to experience a holy life is
by being under grace. However, the relationship between
law and grace is not always so clearly understood, but since
being "under grace" is the basis for living the life under
grace, we must give consideration to this matter of law.[1]

I. THE MEANING OF LAW

Law is defined as "a system of rules or principles for
conduct." This is in complete accord with the meaning of
both the Hebrew and Greek words for the law. The Hebrew
word is *torah*, which comes from a verb which means "to send

out the hand" and consequently "to show, indicate, teach, or instruct." The Greek word is *nomos,* which is derived from the verb that means "to deal out, distribute, dispense, assign, or administer." Thus God's law is His system of rules by which He shows and instructs in His will and administers the affairs of the world. Obviously the definition allows for and even implies that there might be differing systems of rules at various times, depending on what particular aspects or how much of His will God wishes to show at a given time.

A system of rules may be tailored for different times, peoples, or purposes. This is true of all life. When traffic is heavy, speed limits are lowered. At many schools there are regulations for underclassmen which do not apply to juniors and seniors. City families have regulations for their children which rural families do not need. God, too, has administered the affairs of His world under different systems of rule which vary according to time, people, and purpose.

A. *The Law of Nature*

There has always been and will always be in the world a law of nature. It is spoken of in Romans 2:14—"For when the Gentiles, which have not the law, . . . are a law unto themselves." This law contains a revelation of God's eternal power and Godhood (Rom. 1:20) and is sufficiently clear to condemn those who reject that revelation (Rom. 1:19). That particular revelation is not sufficient to save but it is sufficient to condemn. A man who does not receive the teaching which God gives through the law of nature proves that he is unable to receive the additional light necessary to salvation. This law of nature is like first-grade truth; if it cannot be comprehended, there can be no promotion to the second grade. If a man rejects the revelation of God in the law of nature, he fails to qualify for the further revelation which will lead him to Christ.

Apparently this law is not merely objective truth about the nature of God. It also has a subjective effect on the man who recognizes its principles. Paul declares that it is then written on the heart and governs the conduct of the life so that a man's obedience to it is shown in his good works (Rom. 2:14).

B. *The Law of Eden*

If law is a system of rules by which God shows and teaches His will and administers the world, that by which He regulated life in the Garden of Eden may be called law. The Garden itself was administered by the commandment to "dress it and keep it." God's will was shown to Adam and Eve by the positive command to eat freely of every tree with the single exception of the tree of the knowledge of good and evil. Adam's and Eve's obedience could be shown in many ways, and disobedience could be exhibited in only one way. When viewed in light of all the privileges which they had, the single negative restriction respecting the tree of the knowledge of good and evil was a very small one. When viewed from the standpoint that this was the only way in which they could disobey God, it was a very significant matter. But that there was law in Eden is perfectly clear.

C. *The Law of the Patriarchs*

Even in the patriarchal age there was a specific revelation of God's will. It was so specific that God called it "my charge, my commandments, my statutes, and my laws" (Gen. 26:5). The detail of this we are not told in the record. However, we do know that it must have included regulations concerning worship (Gen. 8:20), homage (Gen. 14:20), honesty (Gen. 12:10 ff.), capital punishment (Gen. 9:6), and eating meat (Gen. 9:3).

D. *The Law of Moses*

The Old Testament contains by far the most revelation concerning the Mosaic Law, both in quantity and in detail. Since this aspect of law will be dealt with thoroughly later, it will suffice here to indicate only briefly its comprehensiveness. By the most common Jewish count it was divided into 613 commandments—365 negative and 248 positive. These commandments were catalogued into families such as worship, priesthood, sacrifices, alms, cleanness and uncleanness, feasts, etc. The Mosaic Law covered every area of life, and it was holy, just, and good (Rom. 7:12).

E. *The Law of Christ*

"For the law was given by Moses, but grace and truth came by Jesus Christ" (John 1:17). This does not mean that there is no law in this age of grace. Quite the contrary is true, for the New Testament Epistles speak of the "perfect law of liberty" (Jas. 1:25), the "royal law" (Jas. 2:8), the "law of Christ" (Gal. 6:2), and the "law of the spirit of life" (Rom. 8:2). It is the commands contained in these Epistles which compose the law of Christ and it will be recognized immediately that there are hundreds of such commands covering every area of Christian living. Not only are these teachings extensive but they are so definite that they may be termed a law. The various categories into which these commandments fall will be discussed in detail below.

F. *The Law of the Kingdom*

The kingdom age will also have law: "And many people shall go and say, Come ye, and let us go up to the mountain of the Lord, to the house of the God of Jacob; and he will teach us of his ways, and we will walk in his paths: for out of Zion shall go forth the law, and the word of the Lord from Jerusalem" (Isa. 2:3). The Lawgiver and the King will be the Judge thus guaranteeing that the law will be enforced with complete righteousness (cf. Isa. 11:4-5). The fact of such law in the kingdom is clear. What the content of that law may be is not so clear. Many have taken the Sermon on the Mount (Matt. 5-7) as the law of the kingdom, and there is undoubtedly truth in so taking it. However, one must distinguish between those things in that sermon which anticipate the setting up of the kingdom, such as the prayer, "Thy kingdom come" (Matt. 6:10), and those things which pertain to millennial conditions when the kingdom is functioning (such as "resist not evil" and "give to him that asketh thee"—Matt. 5:39, 42). Commands which can be placed in the latter category would certainly be part of the law of the kingdom.

On the basis of this discussion we can make the following observations and conclusions:

1. Throughout all time God is an administrator of the world and an instructor in His will. The kind of administration may differ and the content of instruction may vary, but God has law, "a system of rules or principles for conduct," in every age.

2. God's instructions are clear. They may vary in quantity, addressee, or purpose, but they are always clear.

3. Therefore, man is completely responsible before God's law in every age. When he fails he is without excuse, for God's revelation has been clear.

4. Man does fail unless God comes to his aid. In this age He has done this in grace through the work of His Son and the indwelling power of His Spirit.

II. THE LIMITATIONS OF THE MOSAIC LAW

In a previous chapter the law of Moses was discussed in its Old Testament context solely. It has demonstrated that God made gracious provisions for His people in many ways during that period of history. However, the Mosaic Law must now be considered in the light of the grace of God in Christ. It is one thing to view the law when there is no other rule of life under which men are living; it is quite another to see it in the light of the coming of Christ. In so many ways the Mosaic Law is the outstanding feature of the Old Testament. In Jewish theology the entire Old Testament is called *torah,* or law. However, the first five books, the Pentateuch, were placed on a higher level because Moses was supposed to have had a clearer vision of God than other prophets. The legal aspects of the Pentateuch was the law of Moses, and the Ten Commandments were the first part of that code. The New Testament, too, has quite a little to say about the law sometimes quoting its commandments (and all the Ten Commandments are quoted except the fourth concerning the Sabbath), sometimes summarizing its precepts, sometimes speaking of its good points and sometimes of its weaknesses. Some of the cults in Christendom preach salvation through keeping of the law, and undoubtedly many Christians believe that the Mosaic Law has a large place in the sanctifying of the believer. Immediately the questions arise, What is the relationship of the Christian to the law? Of what use is the law today? These questions can be best answered in five propositions.

A. *The Mosaic Law was given as a unit*

A cursory glance at the record of the giving of the law in the book of Exodus will show that the law was given to Israel as a unit. The Ten Commandments are recorded in Exodus 20. Without a break, chapter 21 continues these words: "Now these are the judgments which you shall set before them." The judgments comprise the material to the end of chapter 24. Without a break chapter 25 goes right on with these words: "The Lord spake unto Moses saying, Speak unto the children of Israel and bring an offering." The text continues with the details concerning the tabernacle and its worship. While it is common to divide the law into the three categories, commandments, judgments, and ordinances, as suggested by the scriptural divisions above, nevertheless such dividing must never be allowed to obscure the fact that the law was given as a unit. Neither must these categories be used in order to get the Christian out from under part of the law. It is not uncommon in Christian theology to say that the judgments and ordinances are done away for the believer, but not the Decalogue. This is unscriptural, to say nothing of being illogical, in view of the unitized construction of the law.

This is further emphasized by noticing the penalties attached to certain commands in each of these three categories of the law. One of the commandments required the keeping holy of the Sabbath day. When this was violated on one occasion by a man gathering sticks on that day, the penalty was death by stoning (Num. 15:32-36). One of the precepts in the category of judgments concerned letting the land have its Sabbatical year of rest. For 490 years Israel ignored that command and God settled the account due His land by sending the people into Babylonian captivity where many of them died (Jer. 25:11). One of the regulations in the third category, ordinances, concerned proper worship. This was disobeyed by Nadab and Abihu, who were punished with immediate death when they offered strange fire before the Lord (Lev. 10:1-7). In each of the three instances the punishment for disobedience involved death, even though the violation was of a different part of the law. The commandments concerning the land or worship were no less important nor was punishment less severe than the command concerning the Sabbath, for the law was given as a unit. One might be facetious and remark that it was a shame that Nadab and Abihu were not Christians so they could has discarded all of the law except the Ten Commandments and thus have been spared!

Of course, one recognizes that the law can be divided many ways. In Jewish theology it was divided into 613 separate commandments rather than into three categories. There was no distinction made between commandments pertaining to spiritual matters and those pertaining to material matters. "If religion is anything, it is everything" was the idea. Thus violation of one part was a violation of the whole. Does not James state this in his Epistle? Some people in the synagogues were showing partiality to others, and James decries it on the basis that it disobeys the law to love one's neighbor as oneself (Lev. 19:18; Jas. 2:8). This single violation, he says, makes them guilty of the whole law (Jas. 2:10). This could not be true if the law were not given as a unit.

B. *The Mosaic Law was given to Israel*

Both Old and New Testaments are unanimous in this. "These are the statutes and judgments and laws, which the Lord made between him and the children of Israel in mount Sinai by the hand of Moses" (Lev. 26:46). In Romans 9:4 the recipients of the law are Paul's kinsmen according to the flesh—Jews—"who are Israelites; to whom pertaineth the adoption, and the glory, and the covenants, and *the giving of the law,* and the service of God, and the promises." This is reiterated in Romans 2:14 by contrasting the Jews who received the law with Gentiles who did not. "For when the Gentiles, which have not the law, do by nature the things contained in the law, these, having not the law, are a law unto themselves." The Mosaic Law was given to Israel and Israel only.

C. *The Mosaic Law is done away*

This is the point over which most stumble, but it should be remembered that this is clearly the teaching of Scripture. Furthermore, to say that the Mosaic Law is done away is not to say that there is no law in the world or that the Christian is free to live as he chooses. There are two important passages which teach that the law of Moses is done away.

The first is Hebrews 7:11-12. In this chapter the writer has been showing that the priesthood of Melchizedek is greater than that of Aaron, and tithing proves it. Abraham gave a tithe of the spoils to Melchizedek, and since Levi, Abraham's great-grandson, out of whom came the Levitical priesthood, also paid tithes on that occasion in Abraham, the whole Levitical priesthood is seen as subordinate to Melchizedek. Then the writer concludes that if the Levitical priesthood could have brought perfection to the people, there would not have been a need for the Melchizedek priesthood (v. 11). "For the priesthood being changed, there is made of necessity a change also of the law" (v. 12). If the priests of Levi could satisfy, we would not need Christ. And if we need Christ, we must have a Melchizedekan order of priests, for Christ being of the tribe of Judah could never qualify as a Levitical priest. And when the priesthood is changed there is of necessity a change made of the law. Thus if the law has not been done away today, then neither has the Levitical priesthood; and, if this be true, Christ is not our high priest. But if Christ is our high priest, we cannot be under law. Every time we pray in the name of Christ we are affirming that the Mosaic Law is done away.

The second passage is II Corinthians 3:7-11. In some ways this passage is stronger, because it is more particular. Here the comparison is made between what was ministered through Moses and what is ministered through Christ. That which Moses ministered is called a ministration of death and it is specifically said to have been written and engraven in stones. What was so written? The Ten Commandments, of course. Thus, this passage declares that the Ten Commandments are a ministration of death. Furthermore, Paul says that they are done away (v. 11), and this specifically applies to the Ten Commandments. Language could not be clearer, and yet there are fewer truths of which it is harder to convince people. Any argument that it is not right or safe to take the Ten Commandments away from people must be directed to Paul and ultimately to the Holy Spirit, who superintended the writing of this passage. If this truth is not believed, there is not much point in proceeding, for this is basic to what follows.

D. *The Mosaic Law has a use*

Even though many things in the Bible are not written directly to us today, they may be usefully applied to us. For instance, just because once long ago God planted a garden and trees but restricted man from eating the fruit of one of those trees, it does not mean that we should all plant similar gardens so that we can prove our obedience to God by not eating the fruit of one of the trees. Neither does it mean that we cannot profit from the lesson which God was teaching Adam and Eve. The Mosaic Law was for Israel and not for Gentiles, and it has now been done away. Nevertheless, we may use it if we do so properly.

That proper use of the law is to show men their utter helplessness and hopelessness before a holy God. "Knowing this, that the law is not made for a righteous man, but for the lawless and disobedient, for the ungodly and for sinners, for unholy and profane, for murderers of fathers and murderers of mothers, for manslayers, for whoremongers, for them that defile themselves with mankind, for menstealers, for liars, for perjured persons, and if there be any other thing that is contrary to sound doctrine" (I Tim 1:9-10). The law is not for righteous men, and we who are in Christ are righteous and therefore not under the law. But the law is for the ungodly to point them to Christ (Gal. 3:19-25). When used this way it is a powerful weapon in the hands of the Spirit of God.

E. *The Mosaic Law has abuses*

The Mosaic Law cannot *save*, and to use it as a means of salvation is impossible and deceiving. It can point to a Saviour but it cannot save. "Therefore by the deeds of the law there shall no flesh be justified in his sight; for by the law is the knowledge of sin" (Rom. 3:20). The church recognized this early in her ministry, for on the first missionary journey Paul declared: "And by him all that believe are justified from all things, from which ye could not be justified by the law of Moses" (Acts 13:39).

Further, the law cannot *sanctify*. This is true for two reasons. First, the law of Moses did not have high enough standards. For instance, the law commanded that they should not take the Lord's name in vain. One can obey this and still be a terrible gossip. The teaching of grace says, "Let your speech be alway with grace, seasoned with salt" (Col. 4:5a), and this covers everything we say. The law requires that we love our neighbors as ourselves (Lev. 19:18), a standard which is human. Our Lord's new commandment insists that we love as He loved us, a standard which is divine (John 13:34). The standards of grace are much higher, and these are the standards required for Christian sanctification.

Second, the Mosaic Law does not provide a sufficient motive. The law said, "Do in order to be blessed"; i.e., "Do because you have to." Grace says, "Do because you have been blessed"; i.e., "Do because you want to." A "have to" motive never produces genuine sanctification. In reality such motivation will actually stir up sin. This was Paul's own testimony: "I had not known sin, but by the law: for I had not known lust, except the law had said, Thou shalt not covet. But sin, taking occasion by the commandment, wrought in me all manner of concupiscence" (Rom. 7:7-8). Dr. H. A. Ironside had a classic illustration of this principle. He told of an old Indian from our great Southwest who took his first train trip to San Francisco. His very first sight of a railroad station was in Albuquerque before he boarded the train. He said to Dr. Ironside, "I looked at the wall and saw a sign that said, 'Do not spit on floor.' Then I looked at floor, and all I saw was spit." Then the man arrived in San Francisco and visited a friend in a lovely home, perfectly furnished with thick carpets, colorful drapes, and beautiful furniture. The old Indian said, "I looked all around. I looked for a sign on the wall. There was no sign saying, 'Do not spit on floor.' I looked on floor, and—no spit."

God wants us to gaze at the riches of His grace in Christ Jesus and let that be our motivation in sanctification. Sometimes Christian leaders have to put up signs because those in their charge for one reason or another do not look at Christ. But the right way to sanctification is by means of a "want to" motivation. And only by believing that we are free from the law with its "have to" requirements can we begin to be sanctified in God's way and meet God's high standards under grace. We are free from the Mosaic Law, but not from law, for we are under "the law of Christ" (Gal. 6:2).

III. THE LAW OF CHRIST

The law of Christ is the "system of rules or principles for conduct" of the Christian today. Although the believer has been set free from the law of Moses, he is nevertheless under law—the law of Christ. Freedom from the law is not lawlessness or license. As Paul put it: "being not without law to God, but under the law to Christ" (I Cor 9:21). It has already been pointed out that the law of Christ is a definite code containing hundreds of specific commandments. To be subject to this law is what it means to be under grace, for the law of Christ is composed of the teachings of grace.

A. *Its Precepts*

The many precepts of the law of Christ may be grouped into four categories.

1. *Positive commands.* Many of the laws in this code are positive guides to action. "Rejoice evermore. Pray without ceasing. In everything give thanks, for this is the will of God in Christ Jesus concerning you" (I Thess. 5:16-18).[2] It is obvious that the New Testament is filled with the positive commands of grace.

2. *Negative commands.* There are, likewise, many negatives in the law of Christ. "And be not conformed to this world; but be ye transformed by the renewing of your mind, that ye may prove what is that good, and acceptable and perfect will of God" (Rom. 12:2).[3] Again it is plain that there are many negative precepts in the law of Christ.

3. *Principles.* Many particulars of Christian conduct must be governed by principles since there are neither positive nor negative commands which specifically apply. Furthermore, it appears that in this complex twentieth century, this non-specific area of conduct is growing larger and larger. The governing principles are clear, however, and they are a vital part of the precepts of the law of Christ. They will be discussed in the next section.

4. *Rules.* For some matters of Christian conduct there are neither definite precepts nor principles. In this area it is necessary to have special rulings. God has made provision for this by giving leaders to His church who rule in these matters (Eph. 4:11-12; I Tim. 3:5). These leaders are given the authority to rule in spiritual matters affecting the lives of their group (Heb. 13:7, 17). The fact that there are rulers obviously means that there are those who are ruled, and in turn the responsibility of the ruled is to obey joyfully (Heb. 13:17). It should be added, however, that rulers may be arbitrary, are not infallible, and may be very negativistic in

their regulations. Moreover, the system of "don'ts" set up by one may conflict with the system of "don'ts" set up by another.

B. *Its Principles*

As indicated above, there are many aspects of Christian conduct which are not governed by specific commandments but by controlling principles. These are guides for those "under the law to Christ" (I Cor. 9:21) in order that they might live in a manner pleasing to Christ.

1. *Is it a weight?* In the twelfth chapter of Hebrews, the writer pictures the Christian life as a race. Having mentioned the instances of faith in the eleventh chapter, and having shown the better things of Christianity, he considers, in the twelfth chapter, what should be the result of proper apprehension of all this truth. He says, "Wherefore seeing we also are compassed about with so great a cloud of witnesses, let us lay aside every weight, and the sin which doth so easily beset us, and let us run with patience the race that is set before us" (Heb. 12:1). We are warned in these verses of the encumbrances of the Christian life, for these are the weights of which the writer speaks. Actually these weights are not sins; they are simply hindrances or encumbrances that impede the runner. In classical Greek the word used here signifies any superfluous weight or burden such as that which results from stoutness or pregnancy.

I have an acquaintance who weighs 240 pounds. I suppose it is all right for a man to weigh that much, but it becomes terribly inconvenient when he tries to do a very simple thing like tying his shoes. His weight then becomes quite a hindrance. Just so, in the Christian life we encounter things which, though not sins in themselves, become hindrances in running the race. It is not against any rule for a runner to carry with him weights as he runs a race in a track meet, but he certainly will not win that way. Any practice in the Chris-

tian race which, although it may be innocent in itself, will
retard the runner, must be laid aside. Remember, too, that
it is only by running that we learn what these things are. As
long as we stand still we will never feel that they are hamper-
ing us. Run, but run stripped of all encumbering weights.

2. *Is it an enslavement?* "All things are lawful unto me, but
all things are not expedient: all things are lawful for me, but I
will not be brought under the power of any" (I Cor. 6:12).
Here again, as with the questions of weights, we are faced
with practices which are not necessarily sins in themselves but
which may become enslaving habits. Literally, things which
are not expedient are things which do not contribute to one's
own benefit, and the criterion for judging the expediency of
things is whether or not those things may become habits. It
is not a question of what harm the practice is, but rather what
good it is. With all our liberty under grace it is so necessary
to walk circumspectly. Therefore, any practice which tends
to become an enslaving habit is something not only of which
a Christian must beware but it is something better left out of
his life altogether. If we, as so many of us are prone to do,
stoutly affirm, that we are not under the power of that thing
which we are practicing, then why not give it up and prove
that this is so?

3. *Is it a stumbling stone?* Not only must the believer consider weights and habits in judging questionable practices,
but he must often limit his liberty by his concern for others—
both believers and unbelievers. In I Corinthians 8, Paul sets
forth the principle that should govern our conduct in relation
to other Christians. It is somewhat difficult to understand
fully the exact situation in which the Corinthian believers
found themselves, but it is evident that there was a question
in their minds of whether or not a Christian was at liberty to
eat meats that had been sacrificed to idols at the time of
slaughter. Possibly such meat was offered at a lower price.

At any rate, they had written Paul asking his advice on the matter. This presented a real dilemma for him. He had to vindicate the principles of grace. He had to avoid offending Jewish feeling. He had to guard against anything that might cause the Gentile Christians to slip back into idolatry. His answer to this problem was this: God is one; therefore, the sacrifice to the idol is an invalid transaction (v. 4). However, he goes on to say, not all have grasped this truth and some are still in a certain sense under the spell of the idol; therefore, for them to eat would be sin. Since this is the case, stronger Christians should abstain from eating such meats for the sake of those weaker brethren (v. 7-13).

The summation of the argument and the great principle of conduct in relation to our Christian brethren is simply this: "Wherefore, if meat make my brother to offend, I will eat no flesh while the world standeth, lest I make my brother to offend." Thus Paul limits liberty by love, a love that is willing to refrain from that which is innocent in itself in order that the weaker brother will not stumble in his walk because of our example. Although the specific problem changes many times, the principle abides. It will be used, too, by those who sincerely love their brethren in the Lord.

4. *Is it winsome?* Not only does God expect certain things of us in relation to our brethren, but He also has fixed certain standards for our relations with the unsaved. Paul commands us to "walk in wisdom toward them that are without, redeeming the time" (Col. 4:5). What this may mean, in each individual believer's case, God must reveal to the individual heart. It will certainly include the principle that we are to give no offense to the unsaved man (I Cor. 10:32). But perhaps we can best specifically define walking in wisdom by considering Paul's own example: "For though I be free from all men, yet have I made myself servant unto all, that I might gain the Jews; to them that are under the law, as under the

law, that I might gain them that are under the law; to them
that are without law, (being not without law to God, but
under the law to Christ,) that I might gain them that are
without law" (I Cor. 9:19-21). This is true Christian liberty
limited by one true Christian love.

This standard is one of the most elusive of precise definition
and yet it is one of the most important, for the unsaved man
is constantly watching the believer, and it is imperative that
he walk in wisdom, difficult as that may be. How encouraging
to remember that the same God who set up the standard has
also promised to provide the wisdom necessary for living up
to it (Jas. 1:5)! Surely the one whose heart is filled with the
love and compassion of Christ will gladly become servant of
all that many may come to know that Saviour.

5. *Does it display God effectively?* This is the great summary principle in Paul's discussion of doubtful things in
I Corinthians. "Whether therefore ye eat, or drink, or whatsoever ye do, do all to the glory of God" (I Cor. 10:31). In
deciding the doubtful, the question of this principle is: Does
this pleasure of practice fit in with the glory of God? Is it
something upon which I can sincerely ask the blessing of God?
There may be some things which are not wrong in themselves
but which are practiced in ungodly places with ungodly
people, participation in which would identify us with the
enemies of Christ.

But what is the glory of God? It is the manifestation of any
or all of His attributes. It is displaying God to the world.
Therefore, things which glorify God are things which demonstrate His character to the world. God is glorified in the believer's life when the believer acts so as to reveal truly the
character of God and His will for man.

C. *Its Power*

It is apparent that the standards of the law of Christ are

not only all-embracing but they are of the highest order. This makes it necessary for the man who would meet them to have more power than he has in himself. God who set the standards has also provided the power in the permanent and powerful indwelling presence of the Holy Spirit.

This is not to say that the Holy Spirit did not aid believers in the Old Testament. Many times the Scriptures speak of the Spirit's being in an Old Testament saint as well as coming upon him (cf. Num. 27:18; Dan. 4:8 for *in*; Judg. 3:10; I Sam. 16:13 for *upon*). However, that there is a difference in His ministry in the New Testament is clear from our Lord's own teaching. In summarizing the Spirit's ministry up to the time of His own ministry He said, "He dwelleth with *(para)* you" (John 14:17). In prophesying the new relationship, Christ declared that the Spirit "shall be in *(en)* you" (John 14:17). This different relationship can further be specified as meaning two distinct things: (1) the Spirit today indwells the believer permanently (in contrast to "coming upon" with the possibility of going away) ; and (2) He indwells permanently *every* believer (which was not true of all Old Testament saints). Permanent indwelling is a proof of salvation (Rom. 8:9) , and universal indwelling (among believers) does not depend on spiritual maturity (cf. I Cor. 6:19). Thus by this new relationship God has provided the power which enables every Christian to keep the high standards of the law of Christ. It does depend, however, on the believer to use this power.

D. *Its Purpose*

The purpose of the law of Christ is sanctification. *Sanctify, saint,* and *holy* are all from the same root word, which means "to set apart." A sanctified person is one who in all areas of his life is set apart to God. He is a holy person and thus one who resembles his heavenly Father (I Pet. 1:16). Thus the purpose of the law of Christ is to make God's people godly or Godlike.

But what is God like? The answer to this is found in His Son, Jesus Christ, for "no man hath seen God at any time; the only begotten Son, which is in the bosom of the Father, he hath declared him" (John 1:18). Since the Son has "exegeted" the Father, sanctification is Christlikeness. The purpose of every positive command, every negative command, each principle, and all the rules is to conform us to the image of Christ. Christlikeness, then, is the proof of obedience to the law of Christ, and the particulars which together form this code for Christian living are not ends in themselves, but they are means to that chief end of man, namely, to glorify God by exhibiting in his own life the life of Christ. Grace teaches, and in so doing reproduces itself in the image of Christ.

In order to help accomplish this end, the Scriptures hold before the Christian the example of Christ as well as the law of Christ. The life of Jesus on this earth was a revelation of God, and it revealed grace as He "exegeted" God (John 1:17-18). It is quite natural to expect, then, that the disciplines of grace include the example of Christ for the believer to imitate (I John 2:6). That imitation is the proof of one's profession as a follower of the Master, and generally speaking "it is His loving self-sacrifice that is to be imitated."[4]

This sacrificial spirit was always and everywhere exhibited by the Lord. In His public life and ministry He always exhibited compassion (Matt. 9:36; 14:14; 15:32; 20:34; Mark 6:34; 8:2; Luke 7:13). His love for people was evident (Mark 10:21; Luke 19:41). He constantly offered to help before being asked (Mark 8:7, 15; 12:15; John 5:6), ministering to both physical and spiritual needs (John 6). He sought people out in order that He might bring God's message to them (Matt. 9:35; 15:10; Mark 1:38; 4:1; 6:2; Luke 4:14), and

His ministry blessed the hearts of His hearers (Luke 24:32).
The secret of such a public ministry is found in the personal
life, and our Lord serves as the perfect example. He knew and
used the Word of God (Matt. 4), and He constantly main-
tained fellowship with His Father through prayer (Matt.
14:23; Mark 1:35; Luke 5:16; 6:12; 9:18, 29; 11:1). This is
the pattern after which the Christian should mold his own
life in order to glorify God.

Obedience to the law of Christ, then, glorifies God by
producing Christlikeness in the believer. All the commands
as well as the principles are for this purpose. When Paul
concludes his longest section on Christian conduct, he summarizes all that he has said in these words: "Whether therefore ye eat, or drink, or whatsoever ye do, do all to the glory
of God" (I Cor. 10:31). But what is the glory of God? Technically it is the manifestation of any or all of His attributes.
More simply, it is showing God off. Glory is showing off.

We speak this way often even today. Some time ago I
witnessed a basketball game which had gone into a second
overtime period to determine the winner of a tied game. My
team was ahead by two points with less than a minute left.
We had the ball and, on orders from the coach, were stalling.
Suddenly to everyone's amazement, one of the fellows shot—
and missed. I asked the coach afterward what had possessed
the player to shoot at that time. He replied that he was a
"glory hound" trying to show off in front of his girl, who was
sitting in the stands. Too many Christians are like that player—showing off self all the time. The opposite should be the
case. We should be showing off the Lord Jesus Christ. This
is glorifying God; this is the high and holy purpose of the law
of Christ; and this is the fruit of the life lived under grace.

4

UNDERSTANDING LEGALISM
AND LIBERTY

LEGALISM AND LIBERTY are two of the most misunderstood concepts related to the Christian life. Because *legalism* is not a biblical word, people understand it to mean various things. *Liberty* is often misunderstood as being the opposite of legalism and at times seems to be equated with license. Since correct thinking about both concepts is absolutely important to wholesome Christian living, in this chapter we turn our attention to these two ideas.

I. WHAT IS LEGALISM?

Legalism is seldom defined though often talked about. A definition is not easy, for legalism is meshed with many other concepts, and a proper definition must be applicable to all cases. In order to arrive at a definition, it is first necessary to define certain other terms and to compare them with and distinguish them from legalism.

A. *Law*

Law has been defined in this book as "a system of rules or principles for conduct." It has been pointed out that several sets of laws have been operative throughout history and that there has been and always will be law in the world. The

73

governing code today is the law of Christ (Gal. 6:2) or, as it is called elsewhere, the "law of the Spirit of life in Christ Jesus" (Rom. 8:2). It is definite, inclusive, and consists of the highest standards.

All of these codes, whether that revealed to Abraham, or Moses, or the believer today, are objective as far as their existence is concerned. None is subjective in this respect, for the code exists regardless of any kind of response or even lack of response to it. *Per se* each code is good, even though a given system may represent a different revelation of God's will for a particular time. Therefore, all the codes—including the Mosaic Law and the Sermon on the Mount—are beneficial to the Christian in helping him to see something of the mind and will of God. But the fact remains, the code itself is an objective entity, and it remains unchanged by my attitude toward it.

This thought leads to an important conclusion. It is this: the existence of a code or law cannot be legalism. The fact that there are regulations, be it those of the Mosaic Law or the law of Christ, is not legalism. Law is not legalism.

B. *Motive*

The second word to think about is motive. Under the Mosaic Law the motive for correct conduct was stated at the institution of that code in these words: "Now therefore, if ye will obey my voice indeed, and keep my covenant, then ye shall be a peculiar treasure unto me above all people; for all the earth is mine: and ye shall be unto me a kingdom of priests and an holy nation" (Exod. 19:5-6a). Simply stated it was this: If you obey, you will be blessed. The illustration of that principle in action was the keeping of the Sabbath day, for God arranged things so that the Israelites should work for six days and then rest on the seventh. The reward of rest followed the duty of labor.

Under the law of Christ the order has been completely reversed. God has blessed believers with all spiritual blessings in the heavenlies in Christ (Eph. 1:3) ; therefore, on the basis of this blessing we are expected to walk worthy of our vocation (Eph. 4:1). Our day of blessing coming as it does at the first of the week reminds us of this principle, and because we are blessed on Sunday, we live to the glory of God for the following six days of the week. The motive for obeying the law of Christ under grace is because we have been blessed rather than in order to be blessed. "But now are ye light in the Lord: walk as children of light" (Eph. 5:8). This is the only proper motive and cannot be changed, reversed, or substituted for. Correct conduct is motivated today by blessings already received. This is an unalterable order. Thus the motive cannot be legalism, though a false motive, a human upsetting of the divine order, may be akin to legalism. One could say that he will live for the Lord in order to be blessed, but since we have already been blessed with all spiritual blessings, no amount of good works can add to that fact. Man's perversion of the true motive then may be closely related to legalism; but since there is only one true motive, then technically the motive cannot be legalism.

C. *Power*

God always gives power to His people to obey His commands. Earlier it was pointed out that many times in the Old Testament it is recorded that the Spirit of God came upon and dwelt in people. Today God has promised to all believers the permanent indwelling of His Spirit. A believer may choose to use, abuse, or disuse that power, but the fact of His presence is an unalterable arrangement of God. No saint today can become disindwelt, for the indwelling of the Holy Spirit in each and all believers is a relationship which is of God's arranging. Thus legalism is not the same as the power. However, it is true that not using the power of the Spirit may be involved in legalistic living (as in Gal. 3:3), but legalism itself is not merely disuse of this power.

D. *Legalism*

The concept of code concerns *what* is involved; the motive concerns *why;* the power, *how.* Legalism is an attitude. Although it involves code, motive, and power, it is basically an attitude. Whereas code, motive and power exist objectively, an attitude is entirely subjective. A legalistic attitude is, of course, directed toward a given code. Its motivation is wrong, and its power is not that of the Spirit. Although legalism is related to these other ideas, still it is primarily an attitude. Legalism may be defined as a "fleshly attitude which conforms to a code for the purpose of exalting self." The code is whatever objective standard is applicable to the time; the motive is to exalt self and gain merit rather than to glorify God because of what He has done; and the power is the flesh, not the Holy Spirit. Legalism may produce outward results very similar to true sanctification, for a legalist is not a non-conformist to the code under which he is living. However, such outward results are at best only counterfeits and can never even approximate genuine sanctification as long as the attitude is legalistic.

E. *Proof*

Let us test this definition in several ways. First, let us test it on a man under the Mosaic Law. Regardless of spiritual condition or ambition, all men under the law had to do certain things in order to maintain their proper relationship to the theocratic commonwealth of Israel. The legalist said, "I have to do what I am supposed to do, and so I will do it to exalt myself." It is the conduct resulting from this kind of attitude which Isaiah so severely condemns (Isa. 1:11-15). It was not the existence of the requirements of the law which produced legalism, but legalism was that fleshly attitude which conformed to those requirements in order to glorify self. On the other hand, the Israelite who was led and motivated by God to bring his sacrifices and offerings, in order to glorify Him who had commanded it, was exhibiting a right attitude.

It cannot be emphasized too strongly that *having* to do something is *not* legalism, but the wrong attitude is. In the example above both Israelites *had* to bring sacrifices; otherwise they would have suffered certain penalties. It was the attitude toward doing what they *had* to do that determined whether or not their action was legalistic. Or to use a non-biblical illustration, a serious athlete has to keep training rules. Most athletes are glad to keep them, rigid as they may be, for the sheer love of the sport. A few conform in order to make the team and glorify, show off, self. The former attitude is love and the latter is legalism, but both attitudes are toward the same rigid code and both result in conformity. Having to conform to a law is not of itself legalism.

Let us test the definition on men under grace. It was pointed out that the teachings of grace may be grouped into four categories. We shall try the definition on an example from each category.

One of the *positive* commands of grace is "Bear ye one another's burdens, and so fulfill the law of Christ" (Gal. 6:2). One of the ways in which this may be done is to obey another positive command, "Pray for one another" (Jas. 5:16). The code requires that we bear one another's burdens by prayer. If I am to meet this standard of the law of Christ I *have* to do this. My motive ought to be that I want to do what I have to do because God has been so good to me, and the power by which I pray effectively is the power of the Spirit. My attitude should be that I can scarcely wait to pray for others in order that God will be glorified in their lives. But my attitude might be that I'll pray for them grudgingly and should any favorable change take place in their lives it will be to my credit and glory—which is legalism. Or if you have a prayer list you can be legalistic about that, if when you are through praying you rise from your knees and entertain the thought, even the fleeting thought, that you are something because you prayed through a long list of names. The attitude toward good things, prayer and a prayer list, has made your prayer time a legalistic self-glorification energized by the flesh. Do not misunderstand. Regularity is not legalism, and spontaneity is not liberty. But the wrong attitude toward regular or irregular times of prayer is legalism.

One of the *negative* commands is "lie not one to another" (Col 3:9). This is a requirement of God's law today. A legalist does not lie in order to be able to boast in the fact that he does not lie. To lie is wrong under any circumstance, but not to do it to exalt self is legalism.

The third category contains those things which must be governed by *principles*. One such principle is not to put a stumbling stone in the path of a brother (1 Cor. 8:13). Some Christians, using this principle, do not attend certain kinds of entertainment. If non-attendance is practiced in order to help others not to stumble and with the sincere motive of glorifying God, then this is a right attitude. If, however, non-attendance is practiced in order to exalt the piety of the one who does not go to such affairs, then this is legalism. However, the opposite course of action may also be legalism. Another Christian may attend in order to prove to all the world that he has liberty, and he is zealous in letting everybody know that fact. Even if it be perfectly all right for him to go, his going and exalting his self-righteous liberty is legalism. He does not go because led of the Spirit and in order to glorify God; therefore, his attendance has become legalistic.

The fourth category consists of those things which are unspecified and concerning which the leaders of the church must make *rules*. Leaders are held responsible under God for making the correct judgments; and those who are being led are responsible to obey. If one obeys in order to show how good he is, then that is legalism. Even obedience in order to get along is legalism. If one obeys, even though he may not agree or understand, in order to obey God and thus to glorify Him, then that is not legalism.

Thus the definition works in all these examples. Legalism is that fleshly attitude which conforms to a code in order to glorify self. It is not the code itself. Neither is it participation or non-participation. It is the *attitude* with which we approach the standards of the code and ultimately the God who authored it.

II. WHAT IS LIBERTY?

Liberty is not the opposite of legalism. We have seen that law is everywhere in the world and in the Bible. We have noticed, too, that legaism is not the law itself, but a fleshly attitude toward whatever standards are in force at a given time. Since legalism is basically an attitude, liberty cannot be the opposite of legalism, for liberty is a position of freedom from restraint. The exact opposite of liberty is slavery (cf. Rom. 6:22; II Pet. 2:19). Christian liberty is the new position in Christ of freedom from the bondage of sin and of the flesh. One can be in this position of liberty and have a fleshly, self-glorifying attitude toward it which would be legalism. Position and attitude are not the same; therefore, liberty is not the opposite of legalism but of slavery or bondage.

A. *The Facets of Christian Liberty*

Christian liberty has several facets to it, which together form the total position into which the believer has been brought in Christ.

1. In Relation to Salvation

The most important component of Christian liberty is the freedom to be able to be justified by faith in Christ. What the law could not do is now free to be done in Christ, for "by the deeds of the law there shall no flesh be justified in his sight" (Rom. 3:20). In Antioch in Pisidia, early in his ministry, Paul preached this freedom to be saved: "And by him all that believe are justified from all things, from which ye could not be justified by the law of Moses" (Acts 13:39). The whole church debated this matter in the first council at Jerusalem (Acts 15:1-35), for some were insisting on circumcision as an addition to faith in order to be saved. In writing of this occasion later, Paul accuses the Judaizers of spying out his liberty "that they might bring us into bondage" (Gal. 2:4). Liberty is the message of the grace of God in Christ; bondage is the use of the law for salvation. This difference between faith and works or liberty and bondage, is the heart of Paul's use of the stories of Sarah and Hagar in Galatians 4:24-31. It was the basis of the Lord's denunciation of the Pharisees: "Then said Jesus to those Jews which believed on him, If ye continue in my word, then are ye my disciples indeed; and ye shall know the truth, and the truth shall make you free. . . . If the Son therefore shall make you free, ye shall be free indeed" (John 8:31-32, 36). The liberty of being justified by faith has freed us forever from the yoke of bondage of the law (Acts 15:10; Gal. 5:1).

2. In Relation to Holy Living

Christian liberty also brings to the believer the freedom to be a slave of righteousness (Rom. 6:18). Such liberty does not place a Christian in the position of being able to live as he pleases; it is not license. It does place him in the position of being able to live as God pleases, a freedom which he did not have as an unregenerate person. This will be developed further below.

3. In Relation to Glorification

The future position of the Christian in glory is also called liberty (Rom. 8:21). This will be shared by the creation also when Christ sets up His kingdom. Notice that again in this passage liberty is contrasted with bondage or slavery. It is the position in which we shall be able to worship and serve God free from the very presence of sin.

In none of these relationships is liberty unrestricted. Justification liberty is not freedom to be saved in any way man may please; sanctification liberty is not license to live as we choose; nor is glorification liberty other than freedom from the bondage of the presence of sin so that we may give wholehearted praise and service to God throughout eternity.

B. *The Limitation of Christian Liberty*

If liberty is not unrestricted, then how is it limited? The answer to this question is particularly important in relation to sanctification, for unrestricted liberty is license, and wrongly restricted liberty is legalism. Rightly restricted liberty is limited by love (Gal. 5:13).

What is love? Usually we think of it as an emotional expression in kind acts. Certainly love is this sort of kindness, but the definition is not inclusive enough. The mother who loves to cuddle her child is quick to express that same love by slapping the little hand that reaches out to touch a hot stove. This act springs from love also, for love is sometimes corrective because it wants to do good. Thus love is doing good to the one loved.

But what is good? The Christian will realize that ultimate good must be linked to the will of God. Good cannot be simply what one or more individuals might desire or think it to be, for such would conflict with others' ideas of good; but good is the outworking of the purposes of God, for all things in His will work together for good. Thus good is the will of God; love is seeking the will of God for the one loved; and Christian liberty must be restricted by such love.

Love-limited liberty will show itself in the believer's actions. This is the basis of the principle of I Corinthians 8:13. Paul answers in the affirmative the question of whether or not Christians could eat meat offered to idols. Since an idol is nothing (I Cor. 8:4), meat offered to nothing could scarcely have been contaminated; therefore, it is quite permissible to eat it. However, he goes on to say, not everyone knows that, and some eat it as though it had been offered to something and thereby contaminated. Thus, although one has liberty to eat, since the exercise of that liberty might stumble a weaker brother, that liberty will gladly be restricted for the sake of a brother's spiritual growth. To eat under these circumstances would be not only a sin (I Cor. 8:12); it would also be legalism, for it would be a gratification of the flesh and a self-glorification in the parading of a perverted liberty.

Love-limited liberty will also manifest itself in the believer's attitude. Too often he can curb his actions without changing his attitude toward the weaker brother whose very weakness restricts the use of his liberty. The wrong attitude is the despising of the weaker brother by the stronger brother (Rom. 14:3a). Likewise, the weaker brother can exhibit a wrong attitude by judging the stronger brother (Rom. 14:3b). We should remember that each of us will have to answer to God for our own actions — not someone else's.

C. *The Power of Christian Liberty*

Christian liberty offers the believer the power to become a servant of righteousness. Liberty is the opposite of slavery, and Christian liberty is the new position of freedom from slavery to sin (Rom. 6:17-22). Notice again that this freedom is not unrestricted, for it is a freedom to become a slave to righteousness. The new position enables the believer to serve God instead of self. Liberty channels the power of God through the life into service for Him.

Paul himself is the best example of this channeling of freedom into service. He testified: "For though I be free from all men, yet have I made myself servant unto all, that I might gain the more. And unto the Jews I became as a Jew, that I might gain the Jews; to them that are under the law, as under the law, that I might gain them that are under the law; to them that are without law, as without law, (being not without law to God, but under the law to Christ,) that I might gain them that are without law. To the weak became I as weak, that I might gain the weak: I am made all things to all men, that I might by all means save some" (I Cor. 9:19-22). This is not an example of "when in Rome do as the Romans do." Paul is not demonstrating two-facedness or multi-facedness, but rather he is testifying of a constant, restrictive self-discipline in order to be able to serve all sorts of men. Just as a narrowly channeled stream is more powerful than an unbounded marshy swamp, so restricted liberty results in more powerful testimony for Christ. The Colorado River is a lazy stream in many places, but where it flows through the gorges of the Grand Canyon it is a fast-flowing, powerful, and often dangerous river. Believers could well learn a lesson from nature relative to their service.

D. *The Product of Liberty*

Liberty limited by love results in true spirituality. One is spiritual when Christ is seen in the life, for the fruit of the Spirit is a portraiture of our Lord (Gal. 5:22-23). And He who had freedom, limited only by the nature of God Himself, voluntarily took upon Himself the restrictions of the form of a servant in order that He might serve humanity. His liberty was limited by love, and "greater love hath no man than this, that a man lay down his life for his friends" (John 15:13).

The servant is not greater than his master. Liberty brings the believer into a position in Christ as one justified by faith. Liberty guarantees a prospect for the future in his deliverance from the presence of sin. Liberty certainly ought to exhibit itself daily in his practice. The life of liberty is a life of service, following the example of our Lord Jesus Christ. "We then that are strong ought to bear the infirmities of the weak, and not to please ourselves. Let every one of us please his neighbour for his good to edification. For even Christ pleased not himself" (Rom. 15:1-3a).

5

SOVEREIGN GRACE AND ITS BLESSINGS

SINCE BOTH OLD AND NEW TESTAMENTS show that grace is unmerited and since grace in the New Testament concerns principally the saving work of Christ, and since grace affects and is related to many areas of life and doctrine, no discussion of the subject would be complete without considering ramifications of these matters under the general title *sovereign grace*.

I. THE MEANING OF SOVEREIGNTY

Chapter 6 will show that the Old Testament concept of grace includes the picture of a king acting in condescending favor toward his subjects. The New Testament everywhere connects in a vital way grace with the saving work of God in behalf of man. Interwoven throughout both Old and New Testaments are the ideas of election, predestination, and God's choice of a people. Since the very act of His choosing results in favor, and since that choice sometimes seems to have overtones of arbitrariness, the grace of God is often conceived of as an arbitrary display of His favor, or what is often called sovereign grace.

But what does sovereignty actually mean? It is not synonymous with omnipotence, nor arbitrariness, nor omniscience, though it is related to all three. The word itself has to do with ruling or reigning, and "sovereign" means "primary or highest."[1] God is sovereign because He is the primary and highest ruler in the universe. Sovereign grace means ruling grace—a picture which the New Testament confirms in such a passage as Hebrews 4:16, where the throne of grace is depicted as the highest court of appeal.

Sovereign grace, however, is not an unlimited concept. If a sovereign is the highest ruler, his sovereignty is limited by himself. In the case of God the exercise of His grace is limited by His own attributes. Since He is holy and righteous, sovereign grace can in no way violate these attributes. Thus the Apostle explains that, though our justification is freely by His grace, it was accomplished "through the redemption that is in Christ Jesus" (Rom. 3:24). In other words, grace provided the gift of Christ, but His death as payment for sin was required by the holiness of God. In this way God can remain just in the display of His grace, for He justifies those who believe in Jesus' atoning death.

Furthermore, the concept of sovereignty must be correlated with the plan of God. Although God eternally existed as a gracious being, nevertheless it was only through His chosen plan that His grace was revealed. This plan is all-inclusive (Eph. 1:11). However, this does not mean that God sustains the same relationship to each part of it or that He does not use a variety of means in accomplishing it. He is to the over-all plan its architect, and as such He has designed every detail of that all-inclusive plan. Nevertheless, just as an earthly architect is not responsible for the error of a carpenter who misses a nail and injures his thumb, so God places the responsibility for human errors on the individual sinner himself.

In addition, God uses a variety of means in the carrying out of His purposes. Some are direct, as in the slaying of Ananias and Sapphira for their sin (Acts 5:1-11). Some are less direct, as in the case of sickness which is the result of natural causes. Some are quite indirect, as the consequences which come to man because of his willful and persistent sin (Rom. 1:18-32). Laws which God establishes are not violated except in some of the miracles. The most saintly is subject to the law of gravity. All must reap what is sown (Gal. 6:7), and to receive the grace of God in salvation requires faith. Though there was a universal display of God's grace in the Incarnation (Tit. 2:11), there can be no personal reception of that grace apart from faith (Eph. 2:8). Thus sovereign grace is subject to the regulations which are a part of the plan of God.

Finally, sovereignty is a purposeful concept. It is not arbitrary (that is fatalism) nor whimsical (that is chance). Its purposefulness is nowhere better seen than in the display of grace. What is loosely called "free grace" is in one sense devoid of responsibility. In order to receive it a man must believe. In order to enjoy it a man must be obedient. The testimony of Paul, the apostle of grace, was that God's purpose in calling him by His grace was "to reveal his Son in me, that I might preach him among the heathen" (Gal. 1:16). Likewise, the works of all believers are foreordained, and the purpose of God's grace working in us is that we walk in those good works (Eph. 2:10). Even Calvin asserted that disobedience was not by God's command. Thus the purpose of grace as far as the Christian is concerned is the producing of good works.

In relation to God, the purpose of sovereign grace is His glorification. His work of predestination and adoption "according to the good pleasure of his will" is for "the praise of the glory of his grace" (Eph. 1:5-6; cf. vv. 12, 14). It is obvious, then, that the concept of sovereign grace, properly understood, cannot include license, for the life in grace is a life of good works which glorify God. Sovereignty never makes wrong right. The wrath of men may be made to praise God

(Ps. 76:10), but wrath remains wrath. Sin is obviously included in God's plan, but sin remains sin (Acts 4:27-28). Responsibility for maintaining good works is an integral part of purposeful sovereign grace.

II. THE CONCEPT OF ELECTION

Sovereign grace is inseparably linked with the doctrine of election, for grace and election find a common denominator in salvation. Election is unto salvation (Eph. 1:5) and salvation is by grace (Eph. 2:8).

In the Old Testament the idea of sovereignty is everywhere evident. King and subjects, potter and vessel, choice and rejection are well-known Old Testament ideas. However, there is not taught even in the potter illustrations absolute, arbitrary omnipotence, but sovereignty in the sense of God's ruling and human responsibility for sin (Jer. 18; Isa. 29; 45:9; 64:8). Too, the doctrine of election in the Old Testament deals primarily with choosing for privileges in this life rather than election to Heaven or Hell. Any choice unto eternal salvation is only indirectly implied (Ps. 30:12; Prov. 21:3; Isa. 43:20; 45:4; 65:9; Neh. 9:7). Cyrus was chosen to execute God's punishment on His people (Isa. 45:1 ff.) and the Servant of the Lord was chosen to suffer for the people (Isa. 42:1 ff.). Just as some were chosen, so some were rejected. Individuals, like Saul (I Sam. 10:24; cf. 15:23, 26), were rejected as well as the nation as a whole (Hos. 4:6; cf. 9:17; Jer. 6:30; cf. 7:29). Everywhere the sovereignty of God and the real responsibility of man are seen side by side in the Old Testament, and the concept of sovereignty is that of highest ruler. God is not revealed as some sort of personified fate, but as an intelligent, loving, holy, and supreme ruler.[2]

In the main the New Testament doctrine of election was expounded by the Apostle Paul. At least eight different words were used to convey the concept of sovereignty. They are:

proorizo, to mark off beforehand (Rom. 8:29-30) ; *proginosko,* to foreknow (Acts 2:23) ; *eklego,* to choose (Eph. 1:4) ; *kletos,* called (Rom. 1:1) ; *protithemi,* to purpose (Rom. 1:13) ; *boule,* will (Acts 13:36) ; *thelema,* will (Eph. 1:11) ; and *eudokia,* good pleasure (Phil. 2:13). Although it is evident that the doctrine is not built on a single word or a few passages, there are three principal passages in Paul's writings in which the subject is discussed. They are: Romans 8:28-30; Romans 9—11; and Ephesians 1:1-11. Without attempting a detailed analysis of these passages, certain outstanding matters should be noted. (1) God's elective work is for the purpose of conforming the believer to the image of Christ. (2) If God could not have exercised His sovereignty no one would have been saved. (3) Predestination glorifies God. The basic viewpoint of the doctrine is always one of amazement that God should save anyone. It is not surprising, then, to find the word *grace* appearing eight times in these passages (Rom. 11:5-6; Eph. 1:2, 6-7). Paul's doctrine does not find its starting point in the question, Why are some lost? but in the question, Why are any saved? And the answer to this question is, By grace to God's glory. The proper effects of the doctrine are best demonstrated by the Apostle's own life, for it was the realization that God had chosen him that motivated his service for Christ (Gal. 1:15-16).

For Paul the doctrine of election was rooted in his concept of the living, sovereign God. He is the eternal (Rom. 16:26), incorruptible (Rom. 1:23), and wise (Rom. 16:26) God who does all things after the counsel of His own will (Eph. 1:11). Because God is the sovereign ruler He can safely allow man the liberty necessary for responsibility, and Paul's conception of election in no way overrides the reality of human responsibility. The single preposition in II Thess. 2:13, "through sanctification of the Spirit and belief of the truth," shows how closely linked in his mind were God's and man's parts in salvation. Everywhere and in all areas of his life the elect man is constantly exhorted to walk worthy of his calling. The unmerited favor of God is not the forced favor of God upon man. Man is still responsible to place himself in the position of recipient of that grace in order that he might be redeemed, and once a child of God he must keep pace with grace for Christian living (Heb. 12:15).

Balance is the great need in considering this doctrine. While one must not lose sight of the reality of responsibility, that responsibility must not obscure the full meaning of grace. Grace concerns origins; responsibility concerns reactions. God originated His plan of salvation and based it entirely on grace (for sinful man could not merit His favor); yet man is entirely responsible for acceptance or rejection of God's grace. Man's responsibility is to see that he does not frustrate the grace of God by substituting works for grace (Gal. 2:21) and not to do despite to the Spirit of grace by rejecting the way of salvation which God's grace has provided (Heb. 10:29). Grace has provided; responsibility gives man the liberty to acquire, ignore, or reject that provision. Election is by grace, and yet man is responsible to make his calling and election sure (II Pet. 1:10). Grace uses the human will by quickening and empowering it to respond to the grace of God.

What has been said does not imply that the doctrine is without problems. The chief problem is that of reprobation. Why did God not include all in salvation? The most direct statements of reprobation are found in Romans 9:18, 21. Usually reprobation is in the nature of God's abandoning man to his evil deeds and just reward. However, the fact that only a certain group are elected by grace does mean that some have been passed by. Nevertheless, this passing by never implies that God delights in the destiny of the wicked, that they are driven against their wills, that election nullifies a "whosoever" gospel, or that any individual can consider himself nonelect and thereby excuse himself for rejecting God's grace in Christ. This and all problems concerning the doctrine can only find their resolution in the ultimate purpose of election, the glorification of God (Eph. 1:1-11). The very meaning of grace precludes the inference that since some do not merit God's grace, others do. Underlying the entire doctrine of election is the plain fact that no one merits God's favor, and therefore that He extends it to any is grace. Grace by its very nature cannot be deserved; thus election is not of deserving people. This is the uniform emphasis of the doctrine of elective grace.

III. THE BACKGROUND OF SIN

Since sovereign grace is undeserved because of sin, we turn our attention briefly to the doctrine of sin. The opposite of grace, unmerited favor, is merited reward. The opposite of sovereign is enslaved. Thus, sovereign grace is displayed not only by positive declaration and action but also by contrast with enslaving sin. This is the force of several Scriptures (Rom. 3:20-21; I Cor. 6:11; Eph. 2:13; I Tim. 1:12-14), but the contrast between sin and grace is particularly sharp in Romans 6:23: "For the wages of sin is death; but the gift of God is eternal life through Jesus Christ our Lord." Indeed, this antithesis is the essence and development of the argument of this entire first part of the Roman Epistle. Paul traces the effects of sin in order that the benefits of grace may stand out in bold relief, and the argument is climaxed in that paragraph of contrasts, Romans 5:12-21. Sovereign grace is displayed against the background of enslaving sin.

Terms denoting evil are numerous in Hebrew. Indeed, there are more words for evil than for good. There are at least eight basic words: *ra,* bad (Gen. 38:7); *rasha,* wickedness (Exod. 2:13); *asham,* guilt (Hos. 4:15); *chata,* sin (Exod. 20:20); *avon,* iniquity (I Sam. 3:13); *shagag,* err

(Isa. 28:7) ; *taah,* wander away (Ezek. 48:11) ; *pasha,* rebel
(I Kings 8:50) . The usage of these words and other words
leads to certain conclusions about the doctrine of sin in the
Old Testament. (1) Sin was conceived of as fundamentally
being disobedience to God. (2) While disobedience involved both positive and negative ideas, the emphasis was
definitely on the positive commission of wrong and not the
negative omission of good. In other words, sin was not simply
missing the mark, but hitting the wrong mark. (3) Sin may
take many forms, and the Israelite was aware of the particular
form which his sin did take.

The New Testament uses twelve basic words to describe
sin. They are: *kakos,* bad (Rom. 13:3) ; *poneros,* evil (Matt.
5:45) ; *asebes,* godless (Rom. 1:18) ; *enochos,* guilt (Matt.
5:21) ; *hamartia,* sin (I Cor. 6:18) ; *adikia,* unrighteousness
(I Cor. 6:9) ; *anomos,* lawlessness (I Tim. 1:9) ; *parabates,*
transgression (Rom. 5:14) ; *agnoein,* to be ignorant (Rom.
1:13) ; *planan,* to go astray (I Cor. 6:9) ; *paraptomai,* to fall
away (Gal. 6:1) ; and *hupocrites,* hypocrite (I Tim. 4:2) .
From the uses of these words several conclusions may also
be drawn. (1) There is always a clear standard against which
sin is committed. (2) Ultimately all sin is a positive rebellion
against God and a transgression of His standards. (3) Evil
may assume a variety of forms. (4) Man's responsibility is
definite and clearly understood.

It is against the background of sin that grace is displayed
in the Bible. In the Old Testament, as we have seen, grace
appeared in specific acts of favor on the part of man toward
his fellowman and on the part of God toward man. But
grace was never fully revealed until the coming of Christ.
He is the embodiment of the grace of God and the revealer
of it. Because the uniform testimonies of Scripture, history,
and personal experience are that man is sinful, any favor
which God can show must be by grace. Sin earns death as its

reward unless the unmerited favor of God in the person of Jesus Christ intervenes (Rom. 6:23), and that intervention is twofold: the personal appearance of grace in the Incarnation and the individual reception of grace in salvation.

IV. THE BLESSINGS OF GRACE

Grace received in salvation brings to the believer certain possessions and positions. These privileges which accompany saving grace have been fully listed by L. S. Chafer, and we include here with some revision only an outline of them.[3]

A. *The Blessing of Acceptance*

That the grace of Christ personally received unto salvation brings acceptance with God is expressed in the New Testament in the following ways: (1) redeemed (Rom. 3:24); (2) reconciled (II Cor. 5:19-21); (3) forgiven (Rom. 3:25); (4) delivered (Col. 1:13); (5) accepted (Eph. 1:6); (6) justified (Rom. 3:24); and (7) glorified (Rom. 8:30).

B. *The Blessing of Enablement*

Enablement for the believer is assured by the following New Testament phrases: (1) under grace (Rom. 6:14); (2) freed from the law (II Cor. 3:6-13); (3) Christ in you (Col. 1:27); and (4) circumcised in Christ (Col. 2:11).

C. *The Blessing of Position*

The Christian's new position as a recipient of grace is described in a variety of ways: (1) members of a holy and royal priesthood (I Pet. 2:5, 9); (2) citizens of Heaven (Phil. 3:20); (3) members of the family of God (Eph. 2:19); (4) a chosen generation, a holy nation, a peculiar people (I Pet. 2:9); (5) adopted (Gal. 4:5); (6) on the rock (I Cor. 3:11); and (7) light in the Lord (Eph. 5:8).

D. *The Blessing of Inheritance*

An inheritance for the believer is also assured by grace. Facets of it are expressed in the following phrases: (1) complete in Him (Col. 2:9-10); (2) possessing every spiritual blessing (Eph. 1:3); (3) blessed with the earnest of the Spirit (Eph. 1:14); (4) heirs of Heaven (I Pet. 1:4).

These are some of the expressions which are used in the New Testament to describe what God provided for the Christian by His grace.

V. THE MOTIVES FOR GRACE

Why does God act in grace? This is a question the full answer to which man cannot give. Nevertheless, there are some clues to God's motives for the display of His grace, particularly in salvation.

At least three motives are indicated in Paul's discussion of the themes of sovereignty, election, and grace in his Epistle to the Ephesians. Indeed, the major headings of this chapter are all dealt with in Ephesians 1—2. Sovereignty, the doctrine of election, and some of the provisions of grace are included in Ephesians 1. In 2:1-3 Paul paints the background of sin against which the grace of God is then displayed. Sin, he states, brings death, enslavement, selfish action, and wrath. The grace of God which brings the believer into a new position and relationship was motivated, first of all, by the love of God (2:4). Great love is always accompanied by unmerited favor, and the love of God for a sinful world prompted the sending of His Son to pay the penalty for sin (cf. John 3:16). God's love for man is the first motive for His acting in grace on behalf of man.

Second, God made provision for man's salvation in order that "in the ages to come he might show the exceeding riches of his grace in his kindness toward us through Christ Jesus"

(Eph. 2:7). "God's supreme motive is nothing less than His purpose to demonstrate before all intelligences,—principalities and powers, celestial beings, and terrestrial beings,—the exceeding riches of His grace. This God will do by means of that gracious thing which He does through Christ Jesus. All intelligences will know the depth of sin and the hopeless estate of the lost. They will, in turn, behold men redeemed and saved from that estate appearing in the highest glory,— like Christ. This transformation will measure and demonstrate the 'exceeding riches of his grace.' "[4]

Third, God acts in grace toward man so that the redeemed person will produce good works. "For we are his workmanship, created in Christ Jesus unto good works, which God hath before ordained that we should walk in them" (Eph. 2:10). Sovereign grace is purposeful, for the life under grace is a life of good works.

Thus, sovereign grace simply means that grace is the supreme and governing principle in God's ordering of the universe. Because "all have sinned and come short of the glory of God" (Rom. 3:23) His sovereign grace is particularly displayed in the saving of an elect people. What He has provided for them is all of grace, motivated by His great love for man, by His desire to display His grace throughout eternity through redeemed human beings, and by His desire to have a people productive of good works in this life.

6

GRACE AS SEEN IN THE
OLD TESTAMENT

IN OUR WORD STUDY in chapter 1, we saw that the principal words for grace in the Old Testament connote the two ideas of condescending favor and covenant relationship. But, although words are the basis of doctrine, words do not always exhaust the doctrine. This is particularly true of the doctrine of grace in the Old Testament. If grace is the condescending favor of God toward man as especially displayed in His covenant relationships with man, then obviously grace in the Old Testament will be seen in the whole series of God's dealing with mankind. Such a concept of grace will clearly be displayed in the whole biblical history. "It is connected in different ways with the *compassion* of God shown to the needy, the oppressed and the downtrodden; with His *patience* in not allowing the axe of a righteous vengeance to hew down the unfruitful tree ere it be seen to be impossible any longer to withhold it; with His *long-suffering* towards the 'vessels of wrath,' or with His *goodness* to all His creatures, both good and evil, in giving to them 'rain from heaven and fruitful seasons.' "[1]

Thus the display of grace in the Old Testament will be seen both in passages where the words are used and in passages which record the patience, goodness, and compassion of God who is "full of compassion and gracious, slow to anger and plenteous in mercy and truth; keeping mercy for thousands, forgiving iniquity and transgression and sin (Exod. 34:6-7).

I. GRACE BEFORE THE LAW

A. *The Garden of Eden*

Whatever term be used to designate the condition of Adam before the Fall, it is evident that he did have a certain enablement or grace from God. In order to try to find a convenient label for this enablement some have made a theological distinction between "image" and "likeness," image being that which was not lost in the Fall and likeness that which was. Image is thus used to designate the "natural gifts" such as intellectual powers, relative freedom of will, and those traits which Adam did not and could not lose and still remain man. Likeness, then, is made to stand for the "supernatural gifts" or immortality and the kind of righteousness and holiness which Adam lost in the Fall. While it is perfectly proper to take a biblical term and use it in a theological sense,[2] it should be recognized that etymologically it is difficult if not impossible to make a distinction between "image" and "likeness." The opening chapters of the Old Testament use the words and prepositions interchangeably (cf. Gen. 1:26-27 with 5:1-3). Even the New Testament fails to recognize an etymological difference, for what man retained even after the Fall is called both image (I Cor. 11:7; Col. 3:10) and likeness (Jas. 3:9). However, these New Testament passages do teach that certain traits in man which were originally given as the gracious gifts of God were not lost, though they were marred, in the Fall.

What were these gifts of God which Adam had received? They were first of all the things that make man man—intellect, sensibility, and will. But they also consisted of that righteous state which Adam had before sin entered, which enabled him to walk fearlessly with God. It was a kind of holiness, but a holiness which was limited in two ways. First, it was a creaturely holiness, for perfect as the unfallen Adam was he was nevertheless a creature, not the Creator. Second, it was an unconfirmed holiness, for Adam had not yet passed the forbidden-fruit test. Thus the gifts of grace God gave to Adam as a man were crowned with this unconfirmed creature holiness. It is this crown which he lost in the Fall.

The Fall, however, not only affected Adam's righteous standing before God, but it also marred the personality of himself the creature. His intellect was darkened (Eph. 4:18), he became insensible (I Tim. 4:2; Rom. 1:26), and his will became enslaved to sin (Rom. 6:17, 20). The loss of these powers was partial; the loss of holiness was complete. Because of these losses, man became even more dependent on the grace of God. Nature too was affected (Rom. 8:18 ff.), and it required the gracious provision of God in order for the earth to produce anything at all to sustain man (Gen. 3:18-19).

B. *The Patriarchal Period*

Adam's sin also affected his posterity. The effects of the Fall permeated the race so rapidly that every imagination of the thoughts of man was only evil continually (Gen. 6:5; 8:21). Yet in the midst of this corruption there were those who found grace in the Lord's eyes. Abel, who brought to God the kind of offering which He had commanded, was righteous in God's sight (Gen. 4:4; Heb. 11:4). Enoch pleased God (Heb. 11:5). Although a word for grace is not found in reference to these two, it is evident that they found acceptance or favor before God.

The word *grace* is first used in the Bible with reference to Noah. "But Noah found grace [*chen*] in the eyes of the Lord" (Gen. 6:8). As a result, he was saved from the flood and became an heir of righteousness (Heb. 11:7). Abraham found grace (*chen*) in the sight of God (Gen. 18:3), and this revelation of the grace of God was connected with the promise of the seed through Sarah. This is why he is called the father of grace (Ecclus. 44:19-21). Grace (*chesed*) was also displayed to Abraham by God in showing a bride for his son Isaac (Gen. 24:27).

Grace (*chesed*) toward Lot was displayed in granting his request to be allowed to flee to Zoar when Sodom was destroyed (Gen. 19:19). Jacob realized his dependence on the grace (*chesed*) of God when he pled for preservation in the meeting with Esau (Gen. 32:10). He also acknowledged the gift of his children as the gracious gift (*chanan*) of God (Gen. 33:5). Particularly the Lord showed His mercy (*chen*) in giving Joseph favor (*chesed*) in the sight of the keeper of the prison (Gen. 39:21). Later in his life he invoked the grace of God on Benjamin (Gen. 43:29). Israel as a nation is said to have been brought up out of Egypt because of the grace (*chesed*) of God (Exod. 15:13), and Moses their leader was chosen because he found grace in the sight of God (Exod. 33:12-17).

The references above particularly reveal grace in the sight of the Lord. In most of these instances it is the word *chesed* which is used to indicate the covenantal relationship of a superior with an inferior. However, during the patriarchal period grace was also found by men in the sight of men, as the following examples show. In none of these references is *chesed* used; generally the word employed is *chen*, unmerited favor. Job sought favor from his friends (Job 6:14; 19:16-17). Laban sought the favor of Jacob (Gen. 30:27). Jacob asked favor of Esau (Gen. 32:5; 33:8, 10). He also requested on the basis of unmerited favor that his body not be buried in Egypt (Gen. 47:29). Esau entreated the favor of Jacob (Gen. 33:15; 50:4). Joseph found favor in the sight of Potiphar in Egypt

(Gen. 39:4), and when the famine pressed upon Egypt he was entreated by the inhabitants of the land that they might find grace in Joseph's eyes (Gen. 47:25).

This last occurrence of the word *grace* shows that people other than Israelites had some conception of the meaning of grace. This is also attested to by the story of Shechem the son of Hamor the prince of the Hivites, who after defiling Dinah, Jacob's daughter, sought grace from Jacob that he would give him Dinah to be his wife (Gen. 34:11).

From this survey of the display of grace in the period before the law, certain conclusions may be drawn:

(1) Evidence of grace in the lives of men is seen, even though a word for grace may not be used in the record, for Adam, Abel, and Enoch all experienced the grace of God. However, generally one of the words is used.

(2) Adam's gifts of grace were either lost or marred in the Fall with the result that man became even more dependent on the grace of God.

(3) During this period grace was found by men in the sight of God and in the sight of their fellow men. However, *chesed* is never used to indicate the favor in the sight of men. *Chesed* is generally used of the grace of God toward men.

(4) Those outside the promised line also had some conception of unmerited favor, though it was limited to that which could be found in the sight of men rather than God.

(5) The fact that God's *chesed* is shown to those in the promised line is indicative of His covenantal relationship with them.

II. GRACE UNDER THE LAW

Law is usually considered the opposite of grace. In one sense this is true, for the law was given by Moses but grace and truth came by Jesus Christ (John 1:17). However, in a strictly etymological sense the antonym of *grace as unde-*

served favor is *merit as earned reward.* Law is opposed to grace in two ways: (1) the period of the law was a time during which men were shut up to the later revelation of grace in Christ and (2) the basic principle by which the law was operative in the lives of men was a merit principle. If grace is that which was revealed in Christ, there was no grace under the Mosaic law. To attempt to see grace under law in this meaning of *charis* is to fail to "seize the true idea of development, and by an artificial system of typology, and allegorising interpretation . . . to read back practically the whole of the New Testament into the Old."[3] On the other hand, grace in the general sense of unmerited favor was displayed under the law even though the basic operating principle of the law was the merit system. To recognize no grace in this sense during the period of the law is erroneous. To examine the specific nature of this unmerited favor in the merit system is the purpose of this section.

A. *Grace in Election*

Grace is a combination of God's sovereignty and favor exercised on behalf of the creature. Grace is obviously not an inalienable right of the creature, since grace is undeserved favor. It must be administered as God wills, not as the creature demands. "Though the term [grace] is not always used, at least not in this sense, the biblical doctrine of the divine sovereignty is therefore a doctrine of divine grace."[4]

God's elective grace under the law is evident in several ways. The very fact that Gentiles were left to walk in their own ways while Israel became the covenant people of God is an act of sovereign grace, which was confirmed by the giving of the covenant at Sinai (Exod. 19:5; Amos 3:2). This made available to Israelites an imposing array of individual blessings on a scale that rivaled those of the Abrahamic covenant. God's graciously elected people were promised (1) a fruitful land (Lev. 26:4-5; Deut. 7:13; 11:14-15) ; (2) safety and peace (Lev. 26:6) ; (3) victory over enemies (Lev. 26:7-8; Deut. 7:16) ; (4) superlative blessing (Deut. 7:14) ; (5) physical health (Deut. 7:15) ; (6) longevity (Deut. 5:33) ; (7) Yahweh as their personal God (Lev. 26:12).

Not only these specific blessings, but the very giving of the law itself made Israel famous among the nations (Deut. 4:6-8; 33:1-4). Lofty as humanly devised codes were (such as the Code of Hammurabi), the keeping of the divinely-given law made Israel infinitely wiser than the other nations. Though wonderfully singled out from among all other nations, Israel certainly had demonstrated in her past actions no qualifications for this undeserved favor. Her promotion to theocratic statehood was an act of grace. ". . . even in the covenant of the law, the *initiative* (the setting up of the covenant, *heqim,* Gen. ix. 9, xvii. 7, etc.) comes from God as an act of grace . . ."[5] Because of this elective initiative the Mosaic covenant "is an act of grace, and hence not a *suntheke,* a bargain between two equal parties, but a *diatheke,* a divinely ordained agreement."[6]

B. *Grace in Restoration*

It is obvious that the Mosaic law was not entirely a merit system, for it was given as an act of gracious election. It continued operative because of repeated acts of gracious restorations. Somehow the claims of a righteous God as revealed in His law and the acts of unrighteous men must be reconciled. Moses, the only person other than Christ called a mediator in Scripture, fulfills the role of mediator and intercessor. At the first breach of the law Moses offered himself as a sacrifice for the sins of the people (Exod. 32:30-32). Though punishment of the people followed, there was also given to Moses the promise of God's presence (Exod. 33:14), the manifesta-

tion of Himself (Exod. 33:23), the renewed tables of the law
(Exod. 34:4), and further revelation of God's nature (Exod.
34:6-7). Law was certainly mixed with grace.

The conquest of Canaan was accomplished by miracles of
grace, but the children of Israel failed to destroy the inhabitants of the land. Nevertheless God continued to deal with
them in grace. The fourteen judges were an overplus of
grace for the five lapses into idolatry. A new age of religious
revival was inaugurated under Samuel. The office of king was
raised up as a bulwark in defense of the righteousness of the
law (I Kings 2:3; I Chron. 22:12-13). Saul, the first king,
failed. David's life was marred by lapses into sin. Solomon's
initial faithfulness was followed by idolatry and unholy living.
During the divided kingdom Israel lived for 250 years under
nineteen wicked kings. Judah's 390 years of existence under
twenty-seven kings was not much better. But in spite of
apostasy God's grace could not be destroyed, because it was
like the love of a devoted husband for an erring wife (Jer.
31:20; Hos. 2:19; Amos 4).

C. *Grace in the Giving of the New Covenant*

The tension between law and grace caused by the apostasy
of Israel and Judah was broken by the announcement of the
new covenant through the prophet Jeremiah (31:31-34).
Thus the grace of God was again displayed through the giving
of this promise of a new age in the midst of the shambles of
the broken law. This new covenant was categorically contrasted by God with "the covenant that I made with their
fathers in the day that I took them by the hand to bring them
out of the land of Egypt" (Jer. 31:32). "The old relationship
between God and His people is not restored, but entirely
recast."[7] The promised blessings included the impartation
of a renewed mind and heart (v. 33; cf. Isa. 59:21), restoration
of the favor and blessing of God (Hos. 2:19-20; cf. Isa. 61:9),

forgiveness of sin (Jer. 31:34b), the indwelling and teaching ministry of the Holy Spirit (Jer. 31:33-34; cf. Ezek. 36:27), material blessing in the land (Jer. 32:41), the rebuilding of the sanctuary in Jerusalem (Ezek. 37:26-27), and peace (Hos. 2:18). All of these blessings of this new covenant are ratified through blood (Zech. 9:11).

Although the new covenant awaits the future coming of the Deliverer (Rom. 11:26-27), the promise of the covenant was given under the Mosaic law. For this reason and because of all the gracious blessings involved in the covenant, the very giving of the new covenant is another display of the grace of God under the Mosaic law.

D. *Grace in Enablement*

Apparently there were not a few Old Testament saints who achieved substantial conformity to the requirements of the law. This was possible because God in His grace provided them with divine enablement. Such provision of enablement is seldom recognized by the dispensational school of interpretation. "The law, being a covenant of works and providing no enablement, addressed itself to the limitations of the natural man."[8] "The divine enablement seemed nil; and the man was left to his own unaided flesh, which thus became a universal demonstration of man's inability to keep the law. . . ."[9] While it is true that there was under the law no universal nor permanent guarantee of the indwelling presence of the Holy Spirit as there is today (cf. John 14:17), it is nonetheless not accurate to say that there was no enablement under the law.

From the very beginning, Israel was not allowed to think or imagine that her privileged position was the result of her own meritorious action; rather, the people were instructed to recognize that this was a gracious gift of God. "But thou shalt remember the Lord thy God: for it is he that giveth thee power to get wealth, that he may establish his covenant which he sware unto thy fathers, as it is this day" (Deut. 8:18). Reliance on the flesh was emphatically discouraged (Isa. 40:29-31; Zech. 4:6-7; Neh. 8:10), and the godly recognized their dependence on the Lord (I Chron. 29:12).

The Old Testament is replete with references to the source of this enabling grace as being God Himself. David confessed that "in thine hand is power and might; and in thine hand it is to make great and to give strength to all" (I Chron. 29:12). He admonished the people to "seek the Lord and his strength, seek his face continually" (I Chron. 16:11). Many other Scriptures attest to the same truth (Job 12:13; Ps. 18:1; 20:1-6; 28:7-8; 29:11; 59:17; 62:7; 68:28, 35; 73:26; 81:1; 84:5; 118:14; 140:7; Isa. 17:10; Jer. 16:19; Mic. 3:8; Hab. 3:19). In some of these instances enablement is directly linked with salvation (Ps. 118:14; 140:7; Isa. 12:2), and it is said to proceed out of the sanctuary of God as well as immediately from the presence of God (Ps. 20:1-6).

The scope of God's gracious enablement was quite extensive. It included the judges Gideon (Judg. 7:10) and Samson (Judg. 16:28), the prophet Micah (Mic. 3:8), the leaders Nehemiah (Neh. 6:9) and Zerubbabel (Zech. 4:6-7), King David (Ps. 89:21), and the Servant of the Lord (Isa. 49:5). "But it must not be thought that enablement is the privilege of the exceptional few. In Jehovah's hand is power to give strength to all (I Chron. 29:12), particularly those who are the seed of Israel, the children of Jacob (I Chron. 16:11-13), since they are His righteous saints (Ps. 27:14; 31:24) and servants (Ps. 86:16), who may be needy and faint (Isa. 40:29-31; Ps. 73:26) or languishing (Ps. 41:3)."[10] This enablement is sometimes attributed to the work of the Holy Spirit. The Spirit is said to have indwelt certain men in this period like Joshua (Num. 27:18), Daniel (Dan. 4:8; 5:11-14; 6:3), and the prophets (I Pet. 1:11). In more instances He came upon people for enablement (Judg. 3:10; 6:34; 11:29; 13:25; I Sam 10:9-10; 16:13), and in some cases He filled some (Exod. 31:3; 35:31). He provided wisdom (Num. 27:18; I Sam. 16:13), skill (Exod. 28:3; 31:3), and strength (Judg. 13:25; 14:6). Sauer effectively summarizes the scope of enablement under the law and by the law as the Word of God:

> Therefore even in the Old Testament the prophets and psalmist exult (Ps. 32:11; 33:1; 68:4) over the blessings and life-giving effects of the Law. For them the Law was not only exposure of guilt and a leading on to despair (comp. Rom. 7), but "joy of heart" (Ps. 19:8), "delight" (Ps. 119: 47; 36:9), "bliss" (Ps. 32:1).
>
> "Knowledge of sin," says Paul (Rom. 3:20):
> Of "crowning with grace" speaks David (Ps. 103:4).
>
> "The letter kills," says the apostle (II Cor. 3:6):
> "The law is refreshing" [quickening], says the psalmist (Ps. 19:8).
>
> "Miserable man!" is read in the epistle to the Romans (Rom. 7:24):
> "Blessed is the man," says the Psalter (Ps. 1:1; 32:1).
>
> Of the "curse," the one-time Pharisee speaks (Gal. 3:13):
> "The Lord bless thee," says the high priest (Num. 6:24).[11]

It should be noted that the presence of enabling grace did not soften or lessen the stringent demands of the law. Neither today does the gift of the Holy Spirit lower the requirements of grace. Further, the provision of enablement did not mean that it was always or by everyone appropriated. But that there was provision of gracious enablement under the law is incontrovertible.

E. *Grace in the Name of God*

The most specialized name of God in the Old Testament is that one which is especially connected with the period of the

Mosaic law. According to Exodus 6:3 the revelation of this name—Yahweh—belongs to and is particularly characteristic of the Mosaic period.[12] The passage, however, does not necessarily imply that the name was completely unknown before this time. Indeed, Moses' mother's name was Jochebed (Exod. 6:20), which contains the name in its abbreviated form. Therefore, the knowledge referred to in Exodus 6:3 is experiential knowledge. The Israelites would come to know by the experience of redemption not only the existence of Yahweh but all that He would mean to them. "The name Jehovah had not *been yet understood* by the patriarchs, and they had not the *full experience* of that which lies in the name."[13]

What does the name Yahweh mean? Several theories are offered with regard to its etymology, but the true meaning is derived from Exodus 3:14. "The Hebrews themselves connected the word with *hayah,* 'to be.' In Ex 3:14 'Jeh' is explained as equivalent to *'ehyeh,* which is a short form of *'ehyeh 'asher 'ehyeh,* trd in RV 'I am that I am.' This was supposed the mean 'self-existence,' and to represent God as the Absolute. Such an idea, however, would be a metaphysical abstraction, not only impossible to the time at which the name originated, but alien to the Heb mind at any time. And the imperfect *'ehyeh* is more accurately trd 'I will be what I will be,' a Sem idiom meaning, 'I will be all that is necessary as the occasion will arise,' a familiar OT idea (cf. Isa. 7:4, 9; Ps. 23)."[14] Thus the name means existence, but not static existence or God at rest, but active relationship to His people as shown in His dealings with them. Thus the name also "implies the invariable *faithfulness* of God, which side of the notion of Jehovah . . . is specially emphasized in the Old Testament, to awake confidence in God; cf. passages like Deut. vii. 9, Hos. xii. 6, in connection with ver. 7, Isa. xxvi. 4."[15]

The name Yahweh, then, is no doctrinal abstraction but an experimental reality, because of God's redemptive acts in

behalf of mankind. Henry lists three stages in the manifestation of God's grace as expressed in this name: "Israel's deliverance from Egyptian bondage, Israel's adoption as the nation
of God, and Israel's guidance into the promised land."[16]

Some of the specific acts of Yahweh's grace are these: for
the sake of and in the integrity of His name, Yahweh saves
and delivers (Ps. 106:8; 109:21); He quickens in trouble
(Ps. 143:11); He guides in paths of righteousness (Ps. 23:3;
31:3); He will not forsake His people Israel (I Sam 12:22);
He defers anger of His avenging wrath (Isa. 48:9); He
pardons iniquities (Ps. 25:11; 79:9); He works on behalf of
His own (Jer. 14:7; Ezek. 20:9, 14, 22, 44); He keeps His
covenant (Jer. 14:21); and He hears the prayer of the foreign
proselyte (I Kings 8:41; II Chron. 6:22). The name Yahweh,
which is particularly associated with the Mosaic period, displays the grace of God in that period.

III. GRACE UNDER THE DAVIDIC COVENANT

It has already been pointed out that *chesed,* steadfast loving-
kindness, often involves a covenant relationship, either individual or corporate. In many respects the Old Testament
was a world of covenant, and there existed a close connection
between *chesed* and *berith,* covenant (I Sam. 18:3; 20:3, 14-15;
see also Deut. 7:9, 12; I Kings 8:23; II Chron. 6:14; Neh. 1:5;
9:32; and Dan. 9:14, where *berith* and *chesed* are joined by a
copula). Indeed, *chesed* was related to the Abrahamic covenant (Mic. 7:20), the Mosaic covenant (Exod. 34:6-7), the
new covenant (Jer. 31:3), and in a large way to the Davidic
covenant (Isa. 55:3).

The Davidic covenant was established on the basis of God's
steadfast loving-kindness. "I will be his father, and he shall
be my son. If he commit iniquity, I will chasten him with the
rod of men, and with the stripes of the children of men: But
my mercy shall not depart away from him, as I took it from

Saul, whom I put away before thee" (II Sam. 7:14-15). The grace of God guaranteed that the covenant would never be broken. Disobedience would be punished but God's loyal grace would insure the perpetuity of the covenant (Ps. 89:33-34). Indeed, the covenant is called "the sure mercies of David" (Isa. 55:3), and when contemplating its provisions, the psalmist exults in God's loving-kindness (Ps. 107:1; 136:1-26).

The provisions of the covenant included the building of the temple by Solomon, a seed forever, and the establishment of David's throne or kingdom forever. Each of these was based on the grace of God. At the dedication of Solomon's temple the grace of God was the subject of song (II Chron. 5:13-14; 7:6), of praise (II Chron. 7:3), and of prayer (I Kings 8:23; II Chron. 6:14, 42). The birth of Solomon was recognized by Solomon himself as a fulfillment of the Davidic covenant on the basis of God's great faithfulness (I Kings 3:6; II Chron. 1:8). All agree that the fulfillment of the promised seed is in Christ, and He too is related to the grace of God in the covenant (Ps. 16:5). Further, the establishment of the throne was recognized as based on the grace of God (Ps. 89:3-4), and its future fulfillment is also assured by the steadfast faithfulness of God (Isa. 16:5).

All of this becomes one of the most prominent displays of the grace of God in the Old Testament, for three reasons. First, this area of truth is saturated with uses of the word for grace. Further, the particular word used is *chesed,* which indicates the steadfast nature of the covenant relationship which the merciful and faithful God entered into with David and through David with his descendants. Second, the historical fulfillment of the covenant displays, as all fulfilled prophecy does, the faithfulness of God. The birth of Solomon, the building of the temple, the establishment of the kingdom of Solomon all prove the steadfastness of God's promises. Third, if the steadfast faithfulness of God will not be thwarted (Ps. 89:33), if the covenant will not be altered (Ps. 89:34), if Christ is the ultimate fulfiller of the Davidic covenant, if Christ is not now sitting on David's throne but will return to earth to take up that position (Acts 15:14-17), then this display of God's *chesed* will yet be seen in the future when "the Lord God shall give unto him the throne of his father David ... and of his kingdom there shall be no end" (Luke 1:32-33). The ramifications of this display of God's grace extend into eternity.

IV. GRACE IN SALVATION

To say that Old Testament salvation is a complicated doctrine is axiomatic. Whatever differences exist between various viewpoints, all agree that it involved grace.

On the one hand, dispensationalists have been accused of teaching two ways of salvation. A note in the Scofield Reference Bible declares, "The point of testing is no longer legal obedience as the condition of salvation, but acceptance or rejection of Christ. . . ."[17] On the other hand, covenant theology emphatically proclaims the unity of the plan of salvation in both Testaments: "The plan of salvation has always been one and the same; having the same promise, the same Saviour, the same condition, the same salvation."[18]

It would be erroneous to conclude from these quotations that no dispensationalist affirms the unity of the plan of salvation or that no covenant theologian ever speaks of two ways of salvation. Article V of the doctrinal statement of the Dallas Theological Seminary clearly states that that dispensational school believes that "salvation in the divine reckoning is always 'by grace through faith' and rests upon the basis of the shed blood of Christ." This is a strong disavowal of any concept of two ways of salvation. Berkhof, a covenant theologian, in one place writes, "Grace offers escape from the law only as a condition of salvation—as it is in the covenant of works, from the curse of the law . . ." and in another place, "From the law . . . both as a means of obtaining eternal life and as a condemning power believers are set free in Christ."[19] Another covenant theologian declares positively, "The law is a declaration of the will of God for man's salvation."[20] If the law was a means of salvation, as these covenant theologians say, then, of course, there are two ways of salvation—one by the law and one through Christ.

The strange conclusion that we draw from these statements is simply this: while both dispensationalists and covenant theologians imply in their writings that there are two ways of salvation, both deny such as being a part of their systematic theology. Theologically, both groups disavow the saving efficacy of the law and affirm salvation by grace in all ages.

Although both dispensational and covenant theologies teach salvation by grace, the way each explains it is entirely different. The dispensationalist sees grace in the context of the tests of the various dispensations, whereas the covenant theologian grounds it in the covenant of grace. The dispensational viewpoint is clearly stated by Pettingill: "Salvation has always been, as it is now, purely a gift of God in response to faith. The dispensational tests served to show man's utter helplessness, in order to bring him to faith, that he might be saved by grace through faith plus nothing."[21] The covenant viewpoint is clearly stated in the Westminster Confession: "Man, by his Fall, having made himself incapable of life by that covenant, the Lord was pleased to make a second, commonly called the covenant of grace: wherein he freely offereth unto sinners life and salvation by Jesus Christ, requiring of them faith in him, that they may be saved; and promising to give unto all those that are ordained unto life his Holy Spirit, to make them willing and able to believe."[22] Salvation, according to this, was both provided and mediated through the covenant of grace, which is in effect throughout all ages. In this system the object of faith is the Messiah in both Old and New Testaments: "It was not mere faith or trust in God, or simple piety, which was required, but faith in the promised Redeemer, or faith in the promise of redemption through the Messiah."[23] Dispensationalists reply that this covenant of grace is an a priori approach which yields artificial results. They insist that "it was historically impossible that the Old Testament saints should have had as the conscious objects of their faith the incarnate, crucified Son, the lamb of God, and that the sacrifices depicted the person and work of Christ."[24] In other words, for them the covenant viewpoint is a historically impossible anachronism.

A. *The Place of Faith*

The primacy of faith in salvation in all ages is agreeable to dispensational and covenant theologians alike. Thus the condition of salvation, by faith, was the same in the Old Testament as today. This is easily proved.

Abraham believed in the Lord, and He counted it to him for righteousness (Gen. 15:6). The preposition *in* translates the Hebrew prefix *beth,* which indicates that Abraham confidently rested his faith on God (cf. the similar construction in Exod. 14:31; Jonah 3:5). The use of a prefixed *lamedh* would have been weaker, since it would not introduce the person on which he believed but the testimony to which he assented. "The object of Abraham's faith, as here set forth, was not the promise which appears as the occasion of its exercise; what it rested on was God himself, and that not merely as the giver of the promise here recorded, but as His servant's shield and exceeding great reward."[25] Abraham's faith was in God, not in the contents of the Abrahamic covenant.

The Mosaic covenant also involved the exercise of faith.

"The *law*, by always pointing back *to God's electing grace*, and onward to God's just retribution, as the foundation of the righteousness of the law, presupposes *faith*, *i.e.* such a *trusting submission to the covenant God* as was exhibited in *Abraham's* believing adherence to the Divine promise."[26] This involvement of faith is not, however, by command, for faith is not commanded by the Mosaic law; but it is by implication because the covenant relationship implies that an Israelite must have an attitude of trust toward God. Unless by his conduct an Israelite showed disbelief and was consequently cut off, it is assumed that he would have faith in God under the Mosaic law. The place of the sacrificial system will be discussed below. However, there is no disharmony between faith and works under the law. "Judge me, O Lord; for I have walked in mine integrity: I have trusted also in the Lord; therefore I shall not slide" (Ps. 26:1). "The two members of this verse are parallel to each other. *I walk in mine integrity*, corresponds to, *I trust in the Lord*."[27] Notice too Psalm 4:5: "Offer the sacrifices of righteousness, and put your trust in the Lord." The goal of the education of Hebrew children was "That they might set their hope in God, and not forget the works of God, but keep his commandments" (Ps. 78:7). Trust in God and obedience to the law were completely complementary ideas.

B. *The Object of Faith*

The object of faith was God. This is clearly seen from the Old Testament use of the verb *amen*, to believe. The root signifies "to strengthen, support, hold up."[28] It is sometimes used with the prepositional prefix *lamedh,* in reference to, and sometimes with *beth,* in. Its use with the latter preposition in the following passages makes God the object of this assured confidence: Numbers 14:11; 20:12; Deuteronomy 1:32; II Kings 17:14; II Chronicles 20:20; Psalm 78:22; and Jonah

3:5. In all of these instances, with the exception of the Psalm and the Jonah passage, the covenant name Yahweh is used to indicate the object of faith. The use of Elohim in Psalm 78:22 may be accounted for by the fact that Ephraim had rejected Yahweh in His character as the true God, and thus the people's confidence needed to be reassured by the miracles of power proving God to be the Creator. In Jonah 3:5 the reference is to the heathen populace of Nineveh, who were outside the covenant relation with Yahweh. It is true that in all these references spiritual salvation is not in view (cf. Num. 20:12), but the fact that faith was to be directed toward God is clear.

Although Yahweh is primarily the object of faith in the Old Testament, there are several secondary objects of faith associated with Him. For instance, the prophets are associated with God as proper objects of faith, since they are His representatives. "And they rose early in the morning, and went forth into the wilderness of Tekoa: and as they went forth, Jehoshaphat stood and said, Hear me, O Judah, and ye inhabitants of Jerusalem; Believe in the Lord your God, so shall ye be established; believe his prophets, so shall ye prosper" (II Chron. 20:20). In two instances faith is connected with God's Word and commandments (Ps. 106:24; 119:66). Two other occurrences relate faith to the supernatural works or wonders of Yahweh (Ps. 78:32; Isa. 7:9). But, of course, the prophets, the Word, and the works of God are all so closely linked with God Himself that it may be concluded that the verb *to believe* is always associated with God in the Old Testament.

That God who was the sole object of faith was also the Saviour is apparent in the Old Testament. As Saviour He delivered from enemies (II Sam. 23:3). As Saviour He worked wonders, in which capacity He was unique (Isa. 43:11), inscrutable (Isa. 45:15), omniscient (Isa. 45:21), just (Isa

45:21), holy (Isa 43:3), mighty (Isa 49:26; 60:16), and sympathetic (Isa. 63:8-9). In many passages salvation is attributed to Him (I Sam. 2:1; Ps. 9:14; 20:5; 21:1; 69:13; 70:4-5; 8:57; 106:4; 119:123, 166, 174). Thus God is spoken of as a rock of salvation (Deut. 32:15; II Sam. 22:47; Ps. 89:26), a stronghold of salvation (Ps 28:8), and a horn of salvation (Ps. 18:2).

That this Saviour God was the sole origin of salvation is also established by Old Testament revelation. "Salvation is of the Lord" (Jonah 2:9c); "Salvation belongeth unto the Lord" (Ps. 3:8a). So certain is the fact that God alone is the Saviour that it is made the foundation of the formula for solemn oaths (I Sam 14:39); it is the basis of praise (Jer. 17:14); it is frequently set in sharp contrast with the ludicrous and ineffectual attempts of idols to save (Judg. 6:31; 10:41; Isa. 45:20; 46:7; Jer. 2:27-28; 11:12). "For in the thought of the Old Testament salvation is effected by no human act, but by God alone. Whether salvation is from physical or political servitude . . . or whether it is from sin, it is . . . God's act."[29]

That God was the object of faith, that this God was a Saviour, and that He was the only Saviour is clearly taught in the soteriology of the Old Testament. The question now arises, Did that Old Testament revelation include Christ as the conscious object of faith? From the inductive study already made it would seem that it did not. Furthermore, the two summary statements in the New Testament which deal with forgiveness in Old Testament times indicate the same. Both Acts 17:30 and Romans 3:25 teach that Christ's relationship to forgiveness was unknown in the Old Testament. In addition, there are several specific statements which show the ignorance of Old Testament saints regarding salvation through Christ—John 1:21; 7:40; I Peter 1:11. The Johannine passages show how confused the Israelites were about the entire matter, and this makes it difficult to see how one can say that Old Testament saints exercised personal faith in Christ.

However, certain proof texts are proposed as supporting this contention that Old Testament saints did exercise conscious faith in Christ.

The first is Psalm 16:8-11, compared with Acts 2:30-31. It is alleged from these verses that David foresaw the Messiah. However, what David foresaw and what he spoke of are different. He foresaw that one of his descendants would sit on the throne as Messiah. Foreseeing this, he spoke prophetically of the resurrection of Christ. How much of this prophetic utterance David understood is not indicated, but I Peter 1:11 would seem to signify that David and other prophets were guided by the Holy Spirit to say things pregnant with meaning not patent to themselves as they are to us. However, even if David did foresee the resurrection, it was not to him an act of saving faith but a certain assurance of the fulfillment of the promises of the Davidic covenant. There is not the slightest hint that the resurrection was ever related to the sacrificial death of Christ in this connection.

The second proof text is John 8:56: "Your father Abraham rejoiced to see my day: and he saw it, and was glad." This verse is taken to mean that during his lifetime Abraham had some sort of preview of Christ, either on the occasion of the offering of Isaac or at the miraculous birth of Isaac, or when the three angelic visitors came to him or when he met Melchizedek. What Abraham saw is not clear. It may have been the Incarnation, the two advents, the millennial glory, or simply the general hope which centered in Messiah. In any case the New Testament is clear that what he saw caused him to rejoice and be glad, not to be saved. It is equally clear that he was justified by believing Yahweh of the promises.

The third is Job 19:25-26: "For I know that my redeemer liveth, and that he shall stand at the latter day upon the earth: And though after my skin worms destroy this body, yet in my flesh shall I see God." If this is to be used to prove that there was conscious faith in Christ, "Redeemer" must be equated with the Second Person of the Trinity. This is impossible to do, for when Job appeals to his Redeemer, he does so without even remotely comprehending that He is the Second Person of the Trinity. To say that he did would be an anachronism of the wildest sort.

Thus we are forced to conclude that, although faith was required and the object of that faith was God and some saints had special prophetic revelations concerning God, the content of the faith of Old Testament saints did not include the sacrifice of Christ on Calvary. What part sacrifice had in their concept and life will be discussed in the next section, but "that to satisfy God, God must die, that men might inherit God, to be with God, was incomprehensible under the Old Testament seminal knowledge of the Trinity, the incarnation, and the crucifixion followed by the resurrection."[30]

C. *The Sacrificial System*

In addition to the proof texts just cited, covenant theologians see in the ceremonial law a large gospel emphasis designed to awaken a saving faith in Christ.[31] Therefore, it is necessary to examine the Christological content of the sacrificial system and its relation, if any, to Old Testament salvation.

Generally speaking, there are three views as to the efficacy of the Levitical sacrifices. First, their efficacy extended to full remission of sins but that depended on faith on the part of the offerer, since there was no virtue in the sacrifices themselves except as they prefigured the sacrifice of Christ. The second view holds that the efficacy of the Levitical sacrifices extended merely to the remission of temporal penalties involved in the theocratic government of Israel. Such efficacy was unfailingly exerted in every case where the offering was correctly performed, regardless of the inward state of the offerer. A third view combines these two ideas; that is, the sacrifices themselves were efficacious within the commonwealth of Israel, but when offered in faith they also were efficacious for spiritual salvation. The pertinent facts of the matter are two. On the one hand, the Old Testament does ascribe efficacy to the sacrifices. Over and over it was declared that when they were offered according to the law "it shall be accepted for him to make an atonement for him" (Lev. 1:4; 4:26-31; 16:20-22). Nowhere was there indication given that this efficacy depended on the spiritual state of the offerer. Neither is it implied that the worshiper had to have some understanding of the prefigurative purpose to those sacrifices in order for them to be effective in his case. Apparently there was a real atoning efficacy that belonged to the sacrifices because God so arranged it and not because the offerer was worthy.

On the other hand, the New Testament is equally emphatic in its assertion that "it is not possible that the blood of bulls and goats should take away sin" (Heb. 10:4), and "the law, having a shadow of good things to come, but not the very image of the things, can never with those sacrifices, which they offer year by year continually, make the comers thereunto perfect" (Heb. 10:1).

The resolution of this apparent difficulty lies in distinguishing the primary relationship of sin in the Old Testament from that in the New. Under the law, the individual Israelite was related to God through the covenantal, theocratic arrangement. He was born into this and sustained a relationship to the theocracy regardless of his spiritual state. That is, God's covenant with Israel included a governmental arrangement with God as its head—a theocracy. He could not disenfranchise himself. However, since a theocracy is governed by God, any sin is a governmental as well as a spiritual offense. Thus sin for such a person is to be viewed as "affecting the position and privileges of the offending party as a member of the . . . commonwealth of Israel."[32] Although any individual Israelite could be related to God directly, all were related theocratically. Thus the sacrifices which were brought were efficacious in restoring the offender to his forfeited position as a Jewish worshiper and in thus reconciling him to God as Head of the theocracy. The New Testament citizen does not become related to God by natural birth but only by the new birth. Therefore, his sin is to be viewed in relation to God directly, for he has no relationship to a theocracy. Thus the efficacy of the offering of Christ affects his spiritual standing before God. The writer of the book of Hebrews does not say that sins were not forgiven by the Old Testament sacrifices but that those sacrifices were inadequate to remove absolutely and finally the spiritual guilt of an individual before God. This was done by the death of Christ.

Was this theocratic adjustment the sole purpose of the Levitical sacrifices? Undoubtedly God designed the sacrificial system also for the purpose of pointing the faithful worshiper to a better sacrifice which would deal finally with the entire sin question. This means that any such ulterior efficacy which may be ascribed to the sacrifices did not belong to them as sacrifices but as symbols or prefigurations of a final dealing with sin. However, it must not be assumed that the Israelite understood what this final dealing was. If the Old Testament saint had possessed sufficient insight to the extent of seeing and believing on the finished work of Christ, the sacrifices themselves would have lost much of their practicality; for he would have been able to rest in the clearly understood prospect of a completed atonement and would not have had any conscience of sins every year as the Scriptures say he did. "The Old Testament penitent is conscious of being forgiven, and tastes the blessedness of a state of acceptance with God, but he knows not what has become of the guilt of his sin, or how forgiveness has come to him. He trusts in the mercy of God, and does not trust in vain; but of a great central act of reconciling love he knows nothing."[33]

To sum up: the sacrificial system did have a particularized efficacy in restoring the offerer automatically to his theocratic governmental privileges. It could not deal with sin finally and fully. Nevertheless, the sacrifices were designed as symbols of a final dealing with sin and were intended as a means of eliciting faith on the part of an individual in that final dealing. The object of such faith was God and not specifically Christ, but a man who exercised such faith was redeemed even though the content of his faith was different from that of a saint today. Such a redeemed person would naturally be obedient and faithful in offering the sacrifices, for then as now saving faith produced acceptable works.

V. SUMMARY

The Old Testament contains many displays of the grace of God. We have seen grace exhibited before the Fall, to many of the patriarchs in their time, under the Mosaic law (particularly in enablement), under the covenant made with David, and in the work of salvation throughout the entire Old Testament period.

The principal ways in which God displayed His grace may be summarized as follows: (1) He revealed Himself, to Adam and the patriarchs, as the faithful and sufficient Yahweh, as the enabling one, as the originator and keeper of the Davidic covenant, and as the object of faith unto salvation. Whatever revelation God chose to make of Himself in the Old Testament is of grace. (2) He initiated covenants with man so that there could be fellowship between Himself and His creatures. These covenantal arrangements were acts of grace. (3) He made provision for man's eternal salvation. (4) He bestowed temporal favors on men.

But though there were these displays of grace, the Old Testament picture was like a dark negative as compared to the white positive of the New Testament revelation. It was like a candle in comparison to the sun, for Jesus the Son of God, who is the fullness of grace, was not revealed in the Old Testament. All foreshadowings of Messiah were a faint glimmer of light, for grace and truth came through Jesus Christ at His Incarnation.

Our study is finished though our subject is not exhausted, nor could it be. Throughout all eternity we shall worship and serve the One who incarnated grace, and at the same time we shall always be displays of His grace (Eph. 2:7).

In the meantime, may grace teach us "to say 'No' to ungodliness and worldly passions, and to live self-controlled, upright and godly lives in this present age" (Titus 2:12, NIV) to the glory of Him who has made all grace abound toward us.

The grace of our Lord Jesus Christ be with us all.

NOTES

CHAPTER 1

1. Augustine *De Civitate Dei* X. 29.
2. E. Jauncey, *The Doctrine of Grace* (London: Society for Promoting Christian Knowledge, 1925), pp. 4-5.
3. Cf. N. H. Snaith, *The Distinctive Ideas of the Old Testament* (London: The Epworth Press, 1944), p. 129.
4. *Ibid.*, p. 128.
5. T. F. Torrance, *The Doctrine of Grace in the Apostolic Fathers* (Edinburgh: Oliver and Boyd, 1948), p. 11.
6. R. B. Girdlestone, *Synonyms of the Old Testament* (Grand Rapids: Wm. B. Eerdmans Publishing Co., 1953), p. 107.
7. Since "Jehovah" is not a proper transliteration of the Tetragrammaton, Yahweh will be used throughout this book. The Hebrew *YHWH*, translated LORD or GOD in the King James Version and Jehovah in the American Standard is now commonly being rendered Yahweh by Hebrew scholars.
8. C. H. Dodd, *The Bible and the Greeks* (London: Hodder and Stoughton, 1954), pp. 63-64.
9. W. Gesenius, *Hebrew and Chaldee Lexicon* (New York: Wiley, 1890), p. 293.
10. Snaith, *op. cit.*, p. 97.
11. N. Glueck, "Das Wort *Hesed*," *Beihefte zur Zeitschrift für die Alttestamentliche Wissenschaft*, XLVII (1927), p. 3.
12. Torrance, *op. cit.*, pp. 13-14.
13. C. R. Smith, *The Bible Doctrine of Man* (London: The Epworth Press, 1951), p. 49; cf. I Sam. 2:9; Ps. 31:23; 37:28; Prov. 2:8.
14. Snaith, *op. cit.*, pp. 100-102.
15. What follows is a summary of a section in the excellent dissertation of H. C. Woodring, Jr., "Grace Under the Mosaic Covenant" (Dallas: Dallas Theological Seminary, 1956), pp. 175-187.
16. Hesiod *Works and Days* 65.
17. Aeschylus *Agamemnon* 405-406.
18. Homer *Odyssey* viii. 175.
19. Pindar *Olympia* i. 17-19, 30-32.
20. Euripides *Bacchanals* 534.
21. Euripides *Orestes* 159.
22. Euripides *Medea* 227.
23. Pindar *Olympia* viii. 77-80.

24. Aeschylus *Agamemnon* 1304.
25. Aristophanes *Vespae* 1278.
26. Pindar *Olympia* ii. 11.
27. Plato *Gorgias* 462. C; *Sophist* 222. E.
28. Sophocles *Ajax* 522.
29. Euripides *Alcestis* 842; Homer *Iliad* ix. 316-318; v. 211, 874; ix. 613; Sophocles *Oedipus Coloneus* 635-637.
30. Aristotle *Politics* iii. xi. 39; Hesiod *Works and Days* 190-193.
31. Bacchylides *Poems* iii. 38-39; Pindar *Olympia* i. 75-78.
32. J. A. Robinson, *St. Paul's Epistle to the Ephesians* (London: The Macmillan Company, 1914), p. 221.
33. Jauncey, *op. cit.*, pp. 16-17.
34. *Charis* is used 155 times in the New Testament, 101 of which are by the Apostle Paul.
35. Torrance, *op. cit.*, p. 20.
36. J. T. Thayer, *A Greek-English Lexicon of the New Testament* (New York: American Book Company, 1889), p. 666.
37. Cf. A.S.V., "If I partake with thankfulness . . ."
38. H. A. A. Kennedy, *The Theology of the Epistles* (London: Duckworth, 1919), p. 77.
39. Torrance, *op. cit.*, p. 34.
40. J. B. Lightfoot, *Notes on Epistles of St. Paul* (London: The Macmillan Company, 1895), p. 315.
41. F. J. A. Hort, *The First Epistle of St. Peter* (London: The Macmillan Company, 1898), pp. 25-26.

CHAPTER 2

1. Cf. F. Godet, *Commentary on the Gospel of John* (Edinburgh: T. & T. Clark, 1899), I, 278.
2. J. Moffatt, *Grace in the New Testament* (London: Hodder and Stoughton, 1931), p. 95.
3. *Ibid.*, p. 141.
4. Cf. my discussion of this problem in *Biblical Theology of the New Testament* (Chicago: Moody Press, 1959), p. 163 n.
5. Moffatt, *op. cit.*, p. 231.
6. *Ibid.*, p. 219.
7. The author has discussed the question of the Pauline authorship of the Pastorals in his *Biblical Theology of the New Testament*, pp. 164-166.
8. Moffatt, *op. cit.*, p. 350.
9. C. R. Smith, *The Bible Doctrine of Grace* (London: Epworth Press, 1956), p. 64.

CHAPTER 3

1. For further study of this aspect of the doctrine of grace the reader is referred to the very helpful booklet by Alva J. McClain, *Law and the Christian Believer in Relation to the Doctrine of Grace* (Winona Lake, Indiana: The Brethren Missionary Herald Co., 1954), pp. 1-58.
2. See also Rom. 13:1; I Cor. 11:28; II Cor. 6:17; Gal. 6:2; Eph. 5:22; Phil. 4:9; Col. 4:6; II Thess. 3:13; I Tim. 2:8; II Tim. 4:2; Tit. 2:7; Heb. 10:24; Jas. 1:5; I Pet. 2:21; II Pet. 3:18; I John 2:6; II John 5; III John 11b; Jude 24; and Rev. 2:5.

3. See also I Cor. 6:7; II Cor. 6:14; Gal. 4:13b; Eph. 4:30; Phil. 2:4; Col. 3:21; I Thess. 5:19; II Thess. 3:14; I Tim. 4:7; II Tim. 1:8; Tit. 2:10; Heb. 10:25; Jas. 4:11; I Pet. 3:9; II Pet. 3:8; I John 4:1; II John 10; and III John 11.
4. A. Plummer, *The Epistles of St. John* (*Cambridge Greek Testament*) (Cambridge: Cambridge University Press, 1886), p. 39.

CHAPTER 5

1. W. W. Skeat, *An Etymological Dictionary of the English Language* (Oxford: The Clarendon Press, 1946), p. 584.
2. Cf. C. R. Smith, *The Bible Doctrine of Grace* (London: Epworth Press, 1956), pp. 141-147.
3. L. S. Chafer, *Systematic Theology* (Dallas: Dallas Seminary Press, 1948), III, 234-266.
4. L. S. Chafer, *Grace* (Chicago: Moody Press, 1947), p. 29.

CHAPTER 6

1. E. Jauncey, *The Doctrine of Grace* (London: Society for Promoting Christian Knowledge, 1925), pp. 17-18.
2. Cf. the word *atonement,* which, although it is never used in the New Testament, stands for all that is included in the work of Christ.
3. J. Orr, *The Progress of Dogma* (London: Hodder and Stoughton, 1907), p. 303.
4. F. C. Grant, *An Introduction to New Testament Thought* (New York: Abingdon-Cokesbury Press, 1950), p. 124.
5. G. F. Oehler, *Theology of the Old Testament,* (4th ed.; New York: Funk and Wagnalls, 1892), p. 175.
6. Jauncey, *op. cit.,* p. 24; cf. Gal. 4:24; II Cor. 6:14.
7. C. Von Orelli, *The Prophecies of Jeremiah* (Edinburgh: T. & T. Clark, 1889), p. 241.
8. L. S. Chafer, *Systematic Theology* (Dallas: Dallas Seminary Press, 1948), IV, 247.
9. M. F. Unger, "Law and Grace—a Bible Contrast," *Our Hope,* LV (April, 1949), 607.
10. H. C. Woodring, Jr., "Grace Under the Mosaic Covenant" (Dallas: Dallas Theological Seminary, 1956), pp. 140-41.
11. E. Sauer, *The Dawn of World Redemption* (Grand Rapids: Wm. B. Eerdmans Publishing Co., 1951), p. 133.
12. As has already been suggested, "Jehovah" is an artificial English word used to designate the four Hebrew consonants *YMWH* and the vowels of the Hebrew word *Adonai.*
13. Oehler, *op. cit.,* p. 97.
14. B. B. Warfield, "God," *International Standard Bible Encyclopaedia* (Grand Rapids: Wm. B. Eerdmans Publishing Co., 1952), p. 1254.
15. Oehler, *op. cit.,* p. 95.
16. C. F. H. Henry, *Notes on the Doctrine of God* (Boston: W. A. Wilde, 1948), p. 81.
17. *The Scofield Reference Bible* (New York: Oxford University Press, 1909), p. 1115, note 2.
18. C. Hodge, *Systematic Theology* (London: Thomas Nelson and Sons, 1872), II, 368.

19. L. Berkhof, *Systematic Theology* (Grand Rapids: Wm. B. Eerdmans Publishing Co., 1941), pp. 291, 614.
20. O. T. Allis, *Prophecy and the Church* (Philadelphia: Presbyterian and Reformed Publishing Company, 1945), p. 39.
21. W. Pettingill, *Bible Questions Answered* (Wheaton, Illinois: Van Kampen Press, n.d.), p. 470.
22. Chapter VII, Section 3.
23. Hodge, *op. cit.*, II, 366.
24. Dallas Theological Seminary Doctrinal Statement, Article V.
25. B. B. Warfield, "Faith," *A Dictionary of the Bible*, ed. J. Hastings (New York: Charles Scribner's Sons, 1901), I, 828.
26. Oehler, *op. cit.*, p. 459.
27. E. W. Hengstenberg, *Commentary on the Psalms* (Edinburgh: T. & T. Clark, 1854), I, 441.
28. J. B. Lightfoot, *St. Paul's Epistle to the Galatians* (London: Macmillan, 1902), p. 155.
29. H. H. Rowley, *The Re-Discovery of the Old Testament* (Philadelphia: The Westminster Press, 1946), p. 221.
30. J. B. Payne, *An Outline of Hebrew History* (Grand Rapids: Baker Book House, 1954), p. 222.
31. Cf. Berkhof, *op. cit.*, pp. 612-613.
32. T. J. Crawford, *The Doctrine of Holy Scripture Respecting the Atonement* (Grand Rapids: Baker Book House, 1954), p. 250.
33. H. B. Swete, *The Forgiveness of Sins* (London: The Macmillan Company, 1916), pp. 28-29.